PROFESSIONAL STUDIO TECHNIQUES
PRODUCTION ESSENTIALS

Diane Tapscott ▪ Lisa Jeans ▪ Pat Soberanis

Rita Amladi ▪ Jim Ryan

Contributors

Patrick Ames ▪ Sandy Bozek ▪ Russell Brown

Luanne Seymour Cohen ▪ E. M. Ginger ▪ Barry Haynes

Mike Heth ▪ Karl Kuntz ▪ Mattias Nyman

Jim Rich ▪ Grant Ruiz ▪ Mark Samworth

Mark Siprut ▪ Peter Truskier ▪ Steve Werner

Adobe Press
Mountain View, California

Patents Pending.

Library of Congress Catalog No.: 94-76976

ISBN: 1-56830-124-3

First Printing: October 1994   10 9 8 7 6 5 4 3 2

Printed in the United States of America.

Published simultaneously in Canada.

Published and distributed to the trade by Hayden Books, a division of Macmillan Computer Publishing. For information, address Hayden Books, 201 W. 103 Street, Indianapolis, IN 46290. For corporate, educational, or individual sales information, call Macmillan Computer Publishing 800-428-5331 or 317-581-3500.

Credits

Managing Editor: Diane Tapscott

Authors: Diane Tapscott, Pat Soberanis, Lisa Jeans

Art Director: Lisa Jeans

Designer: Mikyong Han

Cover Design: Lori Barnett

Copy Editor: Pat Soberanis

Editor in Chief: Patrick Ames

Technical Editors: Rita Amladi, Jim Ryan, Chris Holm

Technical Consultants: Peter Truskier, George Jardine, Jim Rich, Bret Waters

Contributors: Sandy Bozek, Russell Brown, Luanne Seymour Cohen, E. M. Ginger, Barry Haynes, Mike Heth, Karl Kuntz, Mattias Nyman, Grant Ruiz, Mark Samworth, Mark Siprut, Steve Werner

Other Contributors: Rob Babcock, Fred Barling, Lyn Bishop, Matt Brown, Gary Cosimini, Don Cutbirth, Don Day, Mark Donohoe, Laura Dower, Ivor Durham, Cheryl Elder, Cal Erickson, Steffen Fanger, Nicole Frees, Erik-Paul Gibson, Rod Golden, Laureena Katz Morton, Julieanne Kost, David Lemon, Elizabeth McEnroe, Cheryl Moreno, Judy Mulvenna, Kate O'Day, Sarah Rosenbaum, Jan Seals, Cindy Stief, Karen Tenenbaum, Eric Thomas, Carol Twombly, Jess Walker

Photography: Apple Computer (p. 47); CMCD, Inc. (pp. 42, 43); Luanne Cohen (p. 16); Digital Stock (pp. 7, 10, 19, 25, 28, 31, 33, 34, 35, 36, 37, 38, 44, 45. 49, 51, 88, 89, 95); Kyoko Dougherty (p. 95); D'Pix (p. 54); Du Pont (pp. 15, 31, 34, 37); Eastman Kodak (pp. 13, 14); Fuji (pp. 10, 17, 21); Curtis Fukuda (p. 15); Barry Haynes (p. 46); Bruce Hodge (pp. 10, 17, 20, 21); ImageVAULT (pp. 24, 25, 31, 36, 39, 40, 49); George Jardine (pp. 12, 13, 15, 16, 22, 83); Henrik Kam (p. 66); David Martinez (p. 4); Doug Menuez (p. 12); PhotoDisc (pp. 11, 23, 31, 32, 35, 37, 38, 39, 40, 41, 42, 43, 48, 50, 66, 76, 82, 84, 86, 93); Joe Quintana (pp. 16, 20); Diane Tapscott (p. 95)

Contents

Introduction

Production Essentials is the third book in the Professional Studio Techniques series from Adobe Press. *Production Essentials* is intended to help designers, production artists, illustrators, photographers, and prepress specialists achieve predictable print reproduction using Adobe software.

In the past, clear lines distinguished the roles of designer, production manager, prepress specialist, and printer; today those lines are blurred with the increasing sophistication of digital hardware and software. *Production Essentials* tells you how to use Adobe programs to perform production tasks once left to highly trained professionals.

Production Essentials leads the reader through the print-production process, from scanning to press proofs, and explains the procedures and technology of each stage. The book offers ways to work more efficiently and techniques for color-correcting images and preparing files for output to film. Numerous tips and technical information can be found in the sidebars of every chapter.

Since the craft of producing four-color images is so complex, *Production Essentials* focuses on the capabilities of Adobe Photoshop™ 3.0, although the features of Adobe Illustrator™ 5.5 are also well represented. In addition, *Production Essentials* offers professional typesetting tips using the Adobe Type Library and shows how Adobe Acrobat™ 2.0 can be used for electronic file distribution. The Appendix provides information on PostScript™ error messages and PostScript Printer Description files that prepress specialists and other production professionals will find invaluable.

Although *Production Essentials* was produced using Adobe software on Macintosh® computers, the techniques in this book can be performed using any computer that runs the required Adobe software. If you are using the software with a computer other than a Macintosh, see the Quick Reference Cards provided with your Adobe programs for the alternative keyboard shortcuts.

Working Efficiently

Developing a Production Plan

Setting Up Your System

Working Efficiently in Adobe Illustrator

Working Efficiently in Adobe Photoshop

Calibrating Your System

Working Efficiently

A key measure of an application program's "performance" is the time it takes to open or save a file, send a file to the printer, or refresh the screen after performing an operation. Optimizing performance is critical to creating an efficient working environment for production, but other factors, such as production plans, are also important.

Developing a production plan; minimizing problems that arise when you work with large, complex files; and general tips for using Adobe products all contribute to working efficiently and are covered in this section. You'll also find an overview of and guidelines for calibrating your system.

Developing a Production Plan

Production is a process made up of interdependent steps. The process begins when a project is initiated and ends when it's delivered to the client. By planning for production from the outset, you'll have fewer problems and more consistent results when you go to press.

Projects designed for printing are not usually produced by one person. Typical projects involve writers, designers, production managers, a scanning source, a prepress vendor, and a printer. Good communication among all these players is necessary if a job is to run smoothly. What follows are some practical production planning tips that will help all the members of your team produce jobs efficiently.

Define objectives. Before you start work on any job, make sure that the objectives of the piece to be produced are defined and agreed upon by all parties. Confusion about key objectives usually leads to missed schedules and additional expenses.

Establish a budget. Determine a budget to help define the design and production choices you'll need to make. For instance, will you buy high-end scans or will desktop scans be suitable?

Develop a schedule. Discuss with all contributors how much time each task will take and build an overall schedule.

Identify roles. Define the roles and responsibilities of all team members. Who will review materials? Who will color-correct digital images or trap illustration files? Vendors need to build this work into their schedules and estimates if you don't do the work yourself.

Determine print specifications. Work with your printer to define paper stock, halftone screens, or special printing needs such as varnishes or custom inks. The choices you make when you start a project will help you make other production decisions later.

Establish film requirements. With the halftone screen for printing determined, you can identify output resolution for film. Decide which type of proofs you'll need and whether you expect to see more than one set. How will files be transported between design/production and the vendor? How many images are in your final piece?

Create file-information documents. Both Adobe Illustrator™ 5.5 and Adobe Photoshop™ 3.0, as well as most page layout programs, let you track certain aspects of a job in a separate file that can be kept with your document files (called File Info in Photoshop and Document Info in Illustrator). Information such as photographer, legal rights, scanning resolution, or fonts used can be included in these files for easy reference. Check your application user guides for details.

Setting Up Your System

The way you set up your system can dramatically affect performance. Macintosh® System 7™ and Microsoft® Windows™ 3.1 both have the capability of using *virtual memory*—hard disk space that can be used for temporary storage of data when physical random access memory (RAM) is insufficient.

Adobe Photoshop has its own version of virtual memory called the *scratch disk* (see the *Adobe Photoshop User Guide*). The drawback of using either type of virtual memory is that the time it takes to read and write files on your hard or scratch disk is much longer than when using only physical RAM. (The Macintosh Quadra allows you to set up a RAM disk that is part of your physical RAM, not a scratch disk. The RAM disk enables applications to launch more quickly but does not improve overall performance within applications.) For the best performance using any graphics product, then, add as much RAM as you possibly can. You can also improve performance by using the following guidelines.

Increase the memory assignment. If you are using a Macintosh, increase the amount of memory you have assigned to the application in its Get Info window (in the File menu). If you are using System 7 and have more than 8MB of RAM, turn on 32-bit addressing (in the Memory control panel) before increasing the memory assignment above 8MB. Photoshop 3.0 requires an equal amount of free scratch disk space as the file size. With Adobe Photoshop, you should always turn off the RAM cache in the Control Panel (with System 6) or set the disk cache in the Memory control panel to its lowest setting (with System 7).

Take full advantage of Adobe Photoshop's virtual memory. If you are using a Windows-based system, set up the virtual memory in Windows (known as the *swap file*) so that it is equal to the amount of installed RAM. This is done in the Windows Control Panel by choosing the 386 Enhanced icon.

If you are running Photoshop under System 7, turn off Apple's virtual memory in the Memory control panel. If you have more than one hard disk drive, assign the scratch disk (under Preferences in the File menu) to the fastest disk drive with the most free space. (See the user guide for details.) Photoshop 3.0 provides precise information on scratch-disk sizes, based on the number of layers and channels in your document. To see these amounts, click the triangle at the bottom of the document window and choose Scratch Sizes from the pop-up menu. The first value shows the size for documents without channels or layers; the second value is for those with layers and channels.

If performance still seems slow, try optimizing the disk using a utility such as Norton Utilities™ or SUM™ (for the Macintosh) or Norton Utilities for Windows. If you are running DOS® version 6.0 or later, type *defrag* at the C: prompt, which automatically optimizes your disk.

Increase the size of the Adobe Type Manager™ font cache. You can significantly speed up type processing by increasing the size of the font cache in the Adobe Type Manager (ATM™) control panel. A larger font cache lets you store more font sizes in memory so that ATM doesn't have to rebuild them each time the screen is redrawn. A larger font cache also enables ATM to generate large sizes that would otherwise display as jagged characters. For most projects, a font cache setting of 320K is sufficient. (See also Chapter 4, "Using Type.")

Set up your fonts carefully. If you are using a Macintosh, you can use a font-management utility such as Suitcase™ to create and manage font suitcases. Because ATM can generate any size typeface from a single font size, you only need to store in your suitcase the sizes you use most often for each type style—usually, 10 points and 12 points for body text, and 36 points and 48 points for display type. On a Windows-based system, you can use FontMinder™ to manage your fonts. (See also Chapter 4, "Using Type.")

Keep the Clipboard clear of large amounts of data. Images and objects on the Clipboard are stored in RAM and can therefore significantly affect performance. To clear the Clipboard of large amounts of data, select a small area of the image you have open and copy the selection to replace the older Clipboard data. In Photoshop, another method is to uncheck Export Clipboard in General Preferences (you won't be able to copy and paste between applications, but you can still save the selection in TIFF or another universal format and import it into another application).

Recommended hardware systems. The charts below show optimal hardware systems that can help you work more efficiently. If you are not in the market for a new system, however, you can maximize performance by adding key components. See "Building a Better System," this page, for more information.

RECOMMENDATIONS FOR PREPRESS SYSTEMS			
COMPONENT	MAC	POWER MAC	WINDOWS*
CPU	QUADRA 950	8100/80	PENTIUM
RAM	256MB	256MB	256MB
VIDEO CARD/ MONITOR	24-BIT/21″	24-BIT/21″	24-BIT/21″
HARD DISK DRIVE	2GB+	2GB+	2GB+
CPU ACCELERATION	YES	YES	YES
VIDEO ACCELERATION	YES	YES	YES
ARCHIVE	YES	YES	YES

RECOMMENDATIONS FOR CREATIVE SYSTEMS			
COMPONENT	MAC	POWER MAC	WINDOWS*
CPU	QUADRA 650-950	7100/66 8100/80	486/PENTIUM
RAM	32MB+	64MB+	32MB+
VIDEO CARD/ MONITOR	24-BIT/21″	24-BIT/21″	24-BIT/21″
HARD DISK DRIVE	500MB–1GB+	1GB+	1GB+
ACCELERATION	YES	YES	YES
TABLET	YES	YES	YES
FILE TRANSFER	YES	YES	YES

Building a Better System

The following points might help you get the most memory, power, and speed you can afford when buying new components.

CPU. Adding a current-model central processing unit (CPU) upgrade board is an easy way to improve performance.

RAM. Install as much RAM as possible in the form of non-composite SIMMs (see also "Increase the Memory Assignment," page 4).

Hard Disk Drives. Drives with the largest capacity aren't necessarily the fastest. Match your budget with a drive that gives you adequate storage space and good throughput performance.

Acceleration. Some accelerator cards boost overall CPU performance; others dramatically increase the redraw speed of graphics applications.

File Transfer. Consider removable cartridges or optical media for transporting large files to outside vendors.

*If you are using Windows NT, you can take advantage of Intel-based machines with multiprocessors, which boost performance significantly when using Adobe Photoshop.

Working Efficiently in Adobe Illustrator

Because the results of most Adobe Illustrator operations are displayed only in Preview mode, most performance issues for Illustrator are directly related to previewing artwork. Once you have set up your system for maximum efficiency, you can minimize the time it takes to preview and print by simplifying your files and by working around complex paths and images whenever possible.

Work with two windows open. You can avoid having to switch back and forth between two views of an illustration by working with two windows open (select Window/New Window). For example, you can work with the windows set at different scales—the first window at Fit In Window, say, with the second at a magnified view. You can also use a second window to display an image in Preview mode while you work in the first window in Artwork mode.

Fit In Window view *Magnified view*

For Macintosh systems, use ⌘-period to cancel previewing. In many cases, a partial preview gives you the information you need to continue with your work. Once Illustrator starts to redraw the screen in Preview mode, you can cancel at any time to return immediately to Artwork mode.

Delete unused patterns and custom colors. In general, it's good practice to delete any patterns and custom colors you are no longer using before you save or print the file. To do this, open the Patterns or Custom Color dialog box (both in the Object menu), click the Select All Unused button, and click Delete. Because the program deletes all patterns or custom colors used in all open files, it's important to make sure that you've closed all other files before performing this operation.

Preview without patterns or placed images. When possible, turn off the Show Placed Images and Preview and Print Patterns options in the Document Setup dialog box (in the File menu). (This applies only to previews of placed bitmapped images in Preview mode.) Remember to turn the Preview and Print Patterns option back on before you print.

Preview selectively. If your file is large or complex, you can dramatically speed up previewing either by selecting an object and using the Preview Selection command (Macintosh, ⌘-Option-Y; Windows, Ctrl-Y) or by hiding the objects you don't need to preview. (To hide all but the selected objects on a Macintosh, press ⌘-Option-3; in Windows, press Ctrl-Alt-3; select Arrange/Show All to see all objects again.) The Layers palette in Illustrator version 5.0 and later is ideal for selective previewing. It lets you create objects on separate layers and view them individually or combine layers and view them together.

Adjust flatness. The flatness setting determines the length, in pixels, of the straight-line segments used to approximate a curve. The higher the flatness, the less accurate the curve but the faster the printing. You can simplify complex paths in an individual object by increasing the flatness setting. For low-resolution devices, a setting of 3 is recommended; for high-resolution devices, a setting of 8 is recommended. In Adobe Illustrator version 5.0 or later, you adjust flatness by changing the Output Resolution value in the Object/Attributes dialog box (see "Setting Flatness" in Chapter 6).

Split paths. Another way to simplify paths is to split them when printing. You can do this by selecting the Split Long Paths option, then entering the highest Output Resolution possible (9600 dpi for version 5.0 and later) in the Document Setup dialog box (version 5.0 and later; for version 3.0, see the user guide). At this resolution, the number of split pieces is maximized, creating the least complex file. The program then splits complex paths based on what the printer's memory can handle. Use this option on a copy of the original file since it can alter the artwork. Also, be sure to turn off the Split Long Paths option immediately after printing; otherwise, it will continue to split all files opened thereafter if those files are saved or printed with the option turned on. (See the user guide for more details.) The Split Long Paths option does not work, however, on stroked paths or compound paths; to simplify these paths, select the path and split it manually using the scissors tool.

Working Efficiently in Adobe Photoshop

Because Adobe Photoshop files can be very large, the key to optimizing performance in Photoshop is finding ways to decrease the size of your files. Once you've done this and set up your system efficiently, you can avoid many performance problems by working on parts of the file individually or by performing certain tasks on smaller, temporary versions of the file. The Quick Edit module in Photoshop 3.0, for instance, allows you to edit a portion of a file without opening the entire file (see the user guide for details).

Set your monitor color to 256 or fewer colors. If you don't need to preview color or if your files are text heavy, set the monitor to 256 colors, gray, or black and white to speed up screen display.

Experiment on a low-resolution version of the file. Often, you can save a lot of time by resampling a copy of the original file at 72 dots per inch and making initial edits and color corrections to this version. Be sure to save the copy of the file under a different name so that you do not inadvertently replace the original. Once you've figured out exactly which features and dialog box values give you the results you want, open the original file and repeat those steps. If you're adjusting color, save the dialog box settings you use for the low-resolution version and then load them with the original file open. Third-party products, such as Daystar's Photomatic,™ allow you to batch-process image editing functions. (See also Chapter 6, "Preparing and Printing Files," and the user guide.)

Make complex selections in Grayscale mode. Because a grayscale image is one-third the size of an RGB image, you can cut processing time by making your selections in Grayscale mode. First, save a copy of the image as a Grayscale file. Then make your complex selection, save the selection to a new channel, and use Duplicate Channels in the Channels palette pop-up menu (in version 3.0) to load that selection into the original image. You can boost the contrast of the grayscale image in the Levels or the Curves dialog box (both under Adjust in the Image menu) to make it easier to select shapes of different colors. Alternatively, select the R, G, or B channel that provides the best contrast and make your selections there.

Save selections and use layers. If you are using Photoshop 2.5 or earlier versions, get in the habit of saving complex selections to channels until you have finished editing a file. This lets you load the selection at any time so that you can easily readjust the area without reselecting. If you have many channels, use Duplicate (Image/Calculate/Duplicate) to copy original channels to another file, then delete them from your

working file so they do not increase that file's size. In Photoshop 3.0, you can isolate parts of a file on separate layers, much as you could with overlays in the traditional production world. By drawing, editing, and pasting on separate layers, you can experiment with and manage file development more easily. (Also see the user guide and Chapter 3, "Color-Correcting and Editing Images," for more information.)

Background layer and Layer 1   *Layer 1 alone*

Work with two windows open. As with Adobe Illustrator files, you can use the New Window command to avoid having to switch back and forth between views of a file. For example, you can work with two windows set at different viewing ratios—the first window at a magnified view, with the second at Fit In Window. Or you can make color corrections to an image while viewing the results in both the composite color channel and an individual color channel of the image.

Apply filters to channels individually. Some Photoshop filters work in RAM only and do not use the scratch disk. If you're having problems running a filter on a color image, try applying the filter to each color channel of the image individually (in the Wave filter dialog box, listed within Distort under the Filter menu, do not click the Randomize button). With this method, you would need only three to five times the *channel* size in assigned RAM rather than three to five times the *entire file* size. Remember that in an RGB image, each channel is one-third the size of the file; in a CMYK image, each channel is one-fourth the size of the file.

Use the shortcuts. As with Adobe Illustrator, you can save time by learning the shortcuts for accessing tools and commands. These are especially useful for operations that you perform all the time such as magnifying (double-click the hand tool to fit an image in the window; double-click the zoom tool to display an image at actual size) and filling a selection with color (on the Macintosh, use Option-Delete to fill with the foreground color and Delete to fill with the background color; on a Windows-based system, use Alt-Delete to fill with the foreground color and Delete to fill with the background color).

Many designers don't operate scanners or imagesetters themselves – or simply don't take the time to calibrate their systems thoroughly. If you fall into this category, at the very least calibrate your monitor to establish a neutral gray and to eliminate any color casts.

Macintosh virtual memory should be used only to allow you to work with more than one application open and to switch between them quickly; do not us it to increase the RAM allocation to Photoshop.

Setting Preferences in Adobe Photoshop

Check Monitor Setup, Printing Inks Setup, and Separation Setup (all under Preferences in the File menu) every time you start a new job. If your printing parameters change–say, your paper stock changes from coated to uncoated–these preferences need to be adjusted. Once you have made the correct settings, consider saving them as a separation table. You can then load the separation table containing the appropriate settings before you separate the image. (For more details, see Chapter 6, "Preparing and Printing Files.")

Calibrating Your System

When a print-reproduction system is fully calibrated, it is possible to evaluate, adjust, control, and optimize an image to achieve predictable results on press. To do this, your scanner, monitor, and imagesetter must agree, both numerically and visually. Ideally, a calibrated system enables scanned-image data to be measured and adjusted accurately on your computer using Adobe Photoshop, then output in identical form from an imagesetter. If your scanner interprets a color as a 50% value, for instance, your monitor should display it as a 50% value and your imagesetter should output a dot that will print a 50% value (after compensating for dot gain on press).

Adobe Photoshop's calibration tools affect how images appear on-screen and determine how Photoshop converts colors from RGB to CMYK. If you have not calibrated your system, you must make color corrections in CMYK mode using densitometer readings from the Info palette in Photoshop. If you try to color-correct visually on a noncalibrated system, the printed piece will not match the image you created on-screen. If you are a beginner or color-correct infrequently, working numerically in CMYK might prove difficult at first. But if you intend to do a lot of color correction yourself, learning to evaluate color by the numbers—that is, if you specify 75% magenta, you should be able to see 75% magenta—is essential.

You can also calibrate Adobe Illustrator version 5.0 or later to match Adobe Photoshop closely by matching Illustrator's calibration settings to those used in Photoshop. In Illustrator, select Color Matching in Preferences under the File menu. In the Color Matching dialog box, turn on CIE Calibration and use the Ink, Monitor, and Gamma settings you used in Photoshop. Once you have Illustrator's calibration settings matched to Photoshop's, the on-screen display of images you import and export between the two applications will be the same. The printed results will always match when you output your separations to film. (For more information, see the *Adobe Illustrator User Guide*.)

If you expect to do accurate color reproduction, you must make sure that the scanners you use capture optimal image data, that your computer monitors read and display the scanned information accurately, and that the imagesetters that produce your film will print on paper exactly what you see on-screen. To do this using Adobe Photoshop:

1. Follow the instructions in the *Adobe Photoshop User Guide* to calibrate your monitor to match a printed proof.

2. To make sure your scanner is providing optimal scans, choose four images—a high key image, a low key image, an average image, and a grayscale image—to run tests on. (See Chapter 3, "Color-Correcting and Editing Images," for more information about image types.) If you only work with a particular type of image (grayscale, for instance), you need only perform tests on that type of image.

3. Depending on your scanner's capabilities, preset your scanner's controls to obtain good dynamic range or Gamma readings. (See "Learning to Use Your Desktop Scanner" in Chapter 2.)

4. Once you've achieved the best scans you can for each type of image (see Chapter 2, "Acquiring Images"), write down the settings you used for future reference.

5. Select Calibration Bars (in Page Setup) and print.

6. Output film from these scans using your imagesetter.

7. To make sure your imagesetter is calibrated, take densitometer readings on the calibration bars from your film. If the readings on the bars are off, you will need to calibrate the imagesetter. Use the calibration tools provided by the imagesetter vendor for the greatest accuracy.

8. Make color proofs from your calibrated film.

9. Compare these proofs to the CMYK image on your monitor; adjust the dot-gain compensation setting to change the on-screen image to match the proof for each image type. Most likely, each image type will look best at slightly different settings. Save these settings in Preferences (see sidebar) and load the appropriate settings for the particular type of image you are working with.

10. Continue to reset preferences in Printing Inks Setup, saving and loading information for each of your image tests. Use these preferences as you work with different types of images.

Acquiring Images

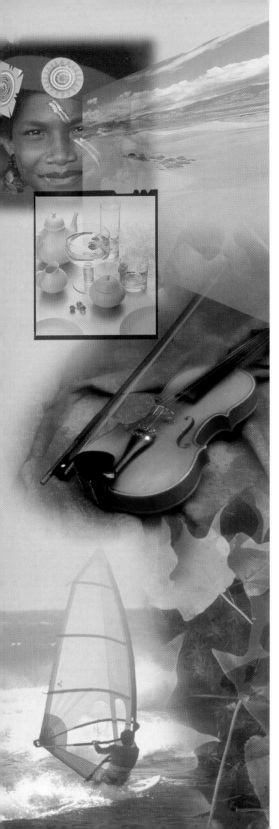

Acquiring Images

Good image reproduction depends on the quality of the digital information you acquire at the outset. And although quality is in the eye of the beholder, a basic understanding of certain aspects of grayscale and color reproduction will help you consistently achieve your desired results.

This section provides an overview of scanners, the scanning process, and the sources from which visual information is digitally acquired. In addition, this section outlines image reproduction concepts that are essential to electronic production, including pixels and bits, file and image size, resolution, resizing, resampling, and interpolation.

Source Images

Traditionally, images prepared for reproduction were classified as line art, which has two tonal values (black and white), or as continuous-tone images, which have the full tonal range in shades of gray or color. Type, rules, and line drawings are examples of line art, while photographs and paintings are examples of continuous-tone art.

Line art   *Continuous-tone image*

Illustration and image editing programs added another category of artwork—digital art—that can be reproduced from digital information that a computer understands. Digital images are classified as either vector or raster. *Vector images,* also called *object-oriented images,* are made up of points on a coordinate system that define straight lines, curves, and type as mathematically determined outlines. *Raster images,* also called *bitmapped images,* are made up of individual bits or pixels of information placed on a grid.

The PostScript™ language lets you create vector images using application programs such as Adobe Illustrator. Vector images are *rasterized* (that is, translated into pixels) by a raster image processor using the PostScript language before they are printed (see Appendix, "Utilizing PostScript"). Adobe Photoshop produces raster images and lets you edit scanned bitmapped images. When you transfer an image from Illustrator to Photoshop, for instance, Photoshop rasterizes Illustrator's vector image. Adobe Streamline™ can convert any image into a vector image (see "Converting Images," page 11).

 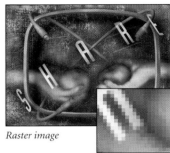

Vector image   *Raster image*

Means of Acquiring Images

You can acquire images for electronic reproduction by scanning existing transparencies or reflective art, by creating electronic art using an application program, by capturing an image using a digital camera, or by accessing a digital image stored on a compact disc.

Transparencies. These positive or negative photographic images must be scanned to convert them into bitmapped information. Because they tend to be sharper and have more vivid color than reflective art, transparencies often produce the most accurate color results.

Reflective art. Photographic prints, paintings, and other artwork that reflects light are known as *reflective art.* As with transparencies, reflective art must be scanned for continuous-tone reproduction.

Electronic art. Images that are created digitally in software programs such as Illustrator, Photoshop, or FreeHand® can be used without conversion in electronic production.

Digital cameras. These cameras capture images in RGB or grayscale directly to disk and require no scanning. They vary greatly in quality, which is closely related to price. At the low end, image resolution is suitable for newsprint, but not for high-quality print reproduction. At the high end, the image information captured compares favorably to that of a good-quality scan.

Compact discs. Compact discs (CDs) are fast becoming popular for storing scanned images that you can access easily through Adobe Photoshop. Two methods are used to get the digital information onto disc. Images are scanned, brought into a computer for further editing, saved in EPS or TIFF format (for example), and then stored on a CD-ROM (compact disc, read-only memory)—a favorite medium for stock photography houses.

Or you can have your 35mm, 4″ × 5″, and other film types scanned and stored directly on a Kodak Photo CD.™ Kodak Photo CD technology allows photo labs to digitize, compress, and store images inexpensively. The regular Photo CD provides five resolutions for each image you supply, with adequate image detail corresponding to thumbnails, for-position-only images, monitor display, printing at small to intermediate sizes (up to 4″ × 5″) at 300 dpi, and printing at larger sizes (such as 8″ × 10″) at 300 dpi. Kodak Pro Photo CD provides a sixth resolution for printing halftones at sizes up to 11″ × 17″ at 300 dpi. (See also "Getting the Best Kodak Photo CD Image," page 24.)

Pixels and Bits

A *pixel* is the smallest picture element displayed on a monitor or read by a scanner. A *bit* is the smallest unit of information a computer recognizes and is used, among other things, to describe a pixel's tonal value. *Bit depth*, also known as *bit resolution*, is a measure of the stored information used to describe each pixel in an image. Common values for bit depth range from 1 bit to 32 bits per pixel.

Bits are similar to electrical switches—they are either on or off. Thinking of bits as switches may help you visualize how they describe color: A bit that is "on" represents black; a bit that is "off" represents white. Each bit, then, has two tonal values—black and white—and is defined mathematically as 2^1. An 8-bit image (2^8) has 256 possible tonal values.

Image bit depth is slightly different than monitor bit depth, which refers to the amount of stored pixel information a monitor is capable of displaying. It is based on the capability of the system's video card. For instance, a 1-bit monitor displays only black and white; an 8-bit grayscale monitor displays 256 shades of gray; while color monitors might have 8-, 16-, or 24-bit display capabilities. Keep in mind that an image's bit depth does not change, regardless of whether it is displayed on an 8-bit monitor or a 24-bit monitor, but that display quality does depend on the monitor type. You can, for instance, display a 24-bit image on an 8-bit color monitor, but the color on the monitor is not as accurate as when you display the image on a 24-bit monitor. For this reason, try to use a 24-bit monitor when you perform critical color adjustments.

A 1-bit image, defined mathematically as 2^1, has two tonal values: white and black.

An 8-bit image, defined mathematically as 2^8, has 256 shades of gray (shown here) or color.

A 24-bit RGB image uses over 16 million colors in three 8-bit channels: red, green, and blue.

An 8-bit monitor displays 24-bit color using a smaller color palette—256 (2^8) or thousands (2^{16}) of colors.

Resolution

The concept of resolution in digital production is somewhat tricky. There are several types of resolution: bit resolution (or bit depth, defined in the previous subsection), monitor resolution, halftone screen resolution, image resolution (also called *scan resolution*), and output resolution. In addition, there are three terms used to define the various resolutions you'll need to reproduce an image: pixels per inch (ppi), lines per inch (lpi), and dots per inch (dpi). (Please note that dpi and ppi are sometimes incorrectly used interchangeably.)

Converting Images

Adobe Streamline converts line art and continuous-tone and raster images into vector images that you can use in different line-art applications and formats, such as Adobe Illustrator, PICT, DXF, and FreeHand. Using Streamline saves hours of time tracing and copying by hand. The resulting files are usually much smaller than their bit-mapped counterparts, which makes them more convenient for archiving and printing. You can convert a single image at a time or quickly convert a large batch of images together. See the user guide for more details.

Raster image

Vector image

Raster image

Vector image

Monitor resolution. Measured in pixels per inch, *monitor resolution* refers to the number of picture elements displayed on a monitor. The resolution of most monitors is fixed, regardless of your image resolution. All Macintosh monitors are 72 ppi, and most PC monitors are 96 ppi. Unless you are working on an image that has exactly the same resolution as your monitor—72 ppi or 96 ppi—the image will appear either larger on-screen than its final output size (the usual case, since your printed output will require image resolutions higher than monitor resolutions) or smaller (occasionally, as for silk-screen printing that uses lower-than-monitor resolutions).

For example, an image with a resolution of 144 ppi will appear twice as large as the output size when viewed on a Macintosh monitor at a 1:1 ratio of monitor pixels to image pixels. If you then scale it to its final output dimensions (1:2 ratio), the pixel information changes on-screen (but not in the file) and the monitor image displays less detail. Any time you make critical image adjustments or need to evaluate an image, as you would a scanned image, you should work at a 1:1 ratio because it is a more accurate representation of your image.

144-ppi image at a 1:1 ratio   *144-ppi image at a 1:2 ratio*

Image resolution. Also measured in pixels per inch, *image resolution* refers to any stored pixel information, such as that recorded by a digital camera or created in an image editing application like Adobe Photoshop. *Scan resolution,* the ppi recorded at the scanning stage, is another type of image resolution.

Halftone screen resolution. Halftone dots used in printing are patterned on a grid. The frequency of lines that make up the halftone screen is measured in lines per inch and is sometimes known as *screen frequency* or *screen ruling* (see Chapter 6, "Preparing and Printing Files"). The printing industry uses standard lpi measurements for different levels of print quality—65–85 lpi for newspapers, for example; and 133, 150, and 175 lpi for magazines and promotional brochures.

85 lpi   *133 lpi*

150 lpi   *175 lpi*

Output resolution. Devices such as laser printers and imagesetters use tiny dots to represent type, line art, and continuous tones. Their output resolution is measured in dots per inch. Laser printers typically print at a resolution of 300–600 dpi, while imagesetters produce output at 1200–6000 dpi. The four images shown here represent the various output resolutions indicated.

600 dpi   *1200 dpi*

2400 dpi   *3000 dpi*

Scanners

The scanning process converts originals such as line and continuous-tone artwork into digital images. Grayscale scanners interpret images in shades of gray, while color scanners capture images in CMYK or RGB mode. To some extent, scanner controls and Adobe Photoshop can compensate for flaws in an original image. However, if critical image details aren't captured during scanning, it's difficult, if not impossible, to achieve good final output. Obtaining a good scan will minimize problems later in the reproduction process.

Scanner Mechanics

Scanners use an optical system, including a light source and filters, to sense tiny spots of image information in the original artwork. This picture data is recorded as pixels onto a grid or bitmap. The number of pixels scanned per inch determines the scanner's image (or scan) resolution. Scan resolution varies by type of scanner from 72 ppi to 9000 ppi. A higher scan resolution indicates that the scanner has recorded more detail, but resolution is only one aspect of a scanner's ability to capture quality information. Dynamic range, recognition of white point and black point, focus, and illumination also affect the quality and accuracy of the digital file captured during scanning.

Dynamic range. The range of discrete tones, from lightest to darkest, a scanner is able to distinguish defines its *dynamic range,* also known as *tonal range.* Certain factors contribute to a scanner's tonal range: its sensors' characteristics, its bit depth, and its ability to convert the information it senses into digital data. For instance, high-end scanners can sense and record the difference between two nearly identical tones. A low-end scanner, however, might record the two similar tones as having the same value, which minimizes the overall tonal variation and alters the contrast of the resulting scanned image. Good tonal range is important for preserving detail and contrast, especially in dark, shadow areas and bright, highlight areas.

Good tonal range   *Poor tonal range*

White-point and black-point recognition. Scanners that cannot recognize and adjust an image's white point and black point (its lightest and darkest points) will not be able to capture subtle tone variations during scanning (see Chapter 3, "Color-Correcting and Editing Images"). This can degrade the scan, resulting in a narrow tonal range and a greater difference between the original and the scanned image.

Good white-point and black-point recognition

Poor white-point and black-point recognition

Scan Resolution

A scanner's maximum image (or scan) resolution – which can be as high as 9000 ppi – is directly tied to its enlargement and reduction capabilities.

Different types of scanners utilize their maximum scan resolutions in different ways. On high-end drum scanners using photo-multiplier sensors, resolution is specified by the job. Enlarging a 4" x 5" transparency five times, to 20" x 25" at 300 ppi, for example, would require a scan resolution of 1500 ppi to achieve the desired quality and would result in a 128MB file in RGB mode.

The number of sensors on a charge-coupled device (CCD) scanner determines its resolution. A CCD scanner with 4096 sensors, for example, has the capability of producing a maximum resolution of 4096 ppi. If the same scanner also has a sophisticated optical system, you could specify resolution by the job, as you can with a high-end drum scanner.

In other CCD scanners, the scanning rate is fixed at, say, 600 ppi. If you needed an output resolution of 300 ppi, however, the scanner's software would adjust the pixel data needed to achieve the 300-ppi output.

You should have the most current version of the scanner software plug-in installed in the Photoshop Plug-Ins folder or the Streamline Plug-Ins folder.

Make sure you use the correct scanning mode. Most scanners offer line-art, halftone, grayscale, and color modes. For instance, to capture the best information for halftone reproduction, you must use either grayscale or color mode – not halftone mode. The halftone scanning mode is intended for output to low-resolution laser printers and does not provide enough levels of gray for high-quality halftone reproduction.

Focusing accuracy. As with camera optics, scanners have apertures that focus the light source on a spot of the original art while the scanner is recording information. The most sophisticated scanners can focus on exactly 1 pixel of information at a time. The less sophisticated optical devices in some scanners might slightly diffuse the light source, resulting in less accuracy. The diffusion tends to soften or muddy the colors and edges in the scanned image. Two scanners with similar resolutions and illumination characteristics, but with different focusing accuracies, may produce scans of radically different quality.

Good focusing accuracy   *Poor focusing accuracy*

Illumination. During the scanning process, it is necessary to maintain consistent illumination from the scanner's light source to achieve accurate scans. Variations in illumination across the image being scanned can produce unwanted artifacts in the digital image.

High-End Scanners

High-end drum scanners use an intense light source, such as a quartz halogen bulb, and a photomultiplier tube to sense image information in an original. This process, known as color separation, divides the scanned information into four digitized channels: cyan, magenta, yellow, and black (CMYK). In addition, these scanners have a full range of image processing tools that let the scanner operator make highlight, midtone, and shadow adjustments and perform color balance, undercolor removal, gray component replacement, selective color correction, and sharpening for better resolution.

When you purchase a high-end scan, it is important to tell the scanner operator what you want from the scan. Do you want the scanned image to match, enhance, or vary from the original? Communicating clearly early on means your image may require little or no additional color adjustment on the computer.

Color separations from a high-end drum scanner can be output directly to film or sent to a computer for editing. If you use high-end scans in your work, your prepress vendor can provide a low-resolution

file to place in your page layout document for position only, or you can get the high-resolution file and make additional adjustments to the image. High-end scanners provide the most accurate pixel information, are expensive to buy and maintain, and are complex to operate; therefore, they are the most expensive way to scan an image.

Desktop Scanners

There once was a clear quality distinction between high-end drum and desktop scanners. Desktop scans usually required additional work at the computer and conversion from RGB to CMYK. With the arrival of desktop drum and more sophisticated desktop flatbed scanners, however, excellent results can now be obtained from desktop scanners.

Most desktop scanners use a fluorescent light source and a sensor known as a charge-coupled device (CCD) to capture image data. Color-control software options vary by manufacturer, but most allow operators to adjust brightness, contrast, and some tonal values.

Low-end CCD scanners provide a narrower dynamic range and less-accurate illumination, focusing, and black- and white-point recognition than high-end scanners do. They might scan reflective art at only 300–600 ppi or capture grayscale or RGB information that must be adjusted, optimized, and converted to CMYK for output using a program such as Adobe Photoshop. These scanners are excellent, however, for images that will be converted into vector images using Streamline.

More sophisticated desktop scanners can scan both reflective and transparent images at higher resolutions. These midrange flatbed and drum CCD scanners provide features similar to those of high-end drum scanners but cost less to purchase and operate.

Choosing the Right Scanner

The key points to consider when choosing a scanner are: the quality of output desired, the subject matter of the image, the final output size, and the skill of the scanning operator. In general, you should consider high-end scanners if you are greatly enlarging a small original, if you need to capture very fine detail, if you need to make color corrections beyond your skill level in Adobe Photoshop, and occasionally if you are printing at halftone screens above 150 lpi.

On the following pages, several types of images are shown that have a wide range of color and image characteristics and have been scanned using high-end drum, midrange flatbed, low-end desktop, and Kodak Photo CD (using the Kodak Acquire module) scanning technologies. Use these as a guide to help you choose the right scanner for your job.

Even slight variations of color in flesh tones are immediately obvious because we intuitively know what skin tones should look like. Some scanners are prone to shifts in color; certain photographic films are as well, especially if shot under incorrect lighting conditions. These deficiencies seem to be more noticeable in flesh tones, where color casts are so easily recognized. Harsh tonal variations in flesh tones result in a garish appearance.

Sky blue, grass green, skin tones, the oranges and reds of fruit, and similar kinds of colors are referred to as known colors *or* memory colors *because most people already have a notion of what these colors look like. The trick to getting an accurate scan of these colors is to match what actually exists in real life.*

An RGB scan of a grayscale image tends to capture a better sampling of tones in its three channels than you would get from a single-channel grayscale scan. This result occurs because the filters and optics in RGB scanners can use the best pixel data from each channel to produce the best grayscale scan.

The reflections in this image create highlights that can be difficult to reproduce; if the highlights fill in during scanning, the image appears flat. Whether grayscale or color, scanning reflections to maintain bright highlights can be difficult.

Reproducing landscape images composed primarily of green and red tones can be difficult because printing inks sometimes contaminate bright, clean greens and reds so they look muddy, especially in the shadow areas. To ensure good results on press, then, it is especially important to capture a wide range of tones during scanning.

Images containing a lot of detail can be problematic to scan because the scanner must discern many distinct jumps in tonal variation to accurately depict the information that appears in the image. High-end scanners are usually best for capturing sufficient pixel data when images have a wide tonal range.

Images with soft edges are not usually difficult to scan; however, these images need to retain their softness during scanning. Doing this requires adjusting the contrast so that distinct shifts don't occur between colors.

HIGH-END DRUM

MIDRANGE FLATBED

LOW-END DESKTOP

KODAK PHOTO CD

Maintaining detail and appropriate contrast in images that are light overall is difficult because the range of tones where detail must be preserved is concentrated in only a portion of the tonal range—the midtone-to-highlight portion. This region should be optimized during scanning. Scanners with less tonal range than others may not produce the best scans of these images.

Scanned images whose main area of interest is concentrated in the midtone region should try to focus details here. Although the highlight and shadow regions may not contain important details, the highlight areas should not become completely white, nor should the shadows become completely black. There should also be a pleasing range of tones, from light to dark.

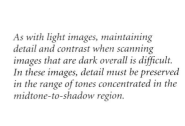

As with light images, maintaining detail and contrast when scanning images that are dark overall is difficult. In these images, detail must be preserved in the range of tones concentrated in the midtone-to-shadow region.

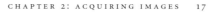

Native Scan Rate

Some desktop scanners work best at their native scan rates. This rate is derived by dividing the image (or scan) resolution by a whole number—the lowest scan resolution being 75. For instance, a 1200-ppi scanner might produce the best scans at a native scan rate of 1200 (1200/1), 600 (1200/2), 400 (1200/3), or a similar derivative.

To use native scan rates, round up your scan resolution to the next highest scan rate. For example, if you are working with a 600-ppi scanner and you determine the scan resolution to be 521 ppi (see "Determining Scan Resolution," page 19), adjust the scan resolution to 600 ppi for optimal scanning results. You will probably need to resize your image in Adobe Photoshop after scanning to attain your desired finished size (see "Interpolation," page 23, for details).

HOW TO MAKE A GOOD DESKTOP SCAN

Capturing the most accurate information you can at the scanning stage will minimize the work you'll need to do later on your computer and will help ensure good final output. Follow these steps to get a good desktop scan:

1. Learn to use your desktop scanner (this page).

2. Evaluate the image characteristics (this page).

3. Set your scanner's controls to minimize deficiencies in the original artwork.

4. Determine the scan resolution (page 19).

5. Optional: Calculate file size (page 19).

6. Make sure the original is dust-free; if necessary, clean the scanning glass.

7. Make sure the original is square on the scanning bed.

8. Scan the image. Make several scans at different settings, recording the settings as you work.

9. If necessary, crop the image in Adobe Photoshop using the cropping tool (see the *Adobe Photoshop User Guide*).

Learning to Use Your Desktop Scanner

Using the instructions that come with your scanner, learn its capabilities by experimenting with its software and mechanical controls.

Learn your scanner manufacturer's terminology; one manufacturer might call a function "midtone adjustment," while another might refer to the same function as "Gamma control." Also, compare the scanner terminology to that used in Adobe Photoshop; again, some terms might vary even when they refer to the same thing.

The following guidelines will also help you learn about your scanner:

1. Scan a variety of test images in different image processing modes, including default and automatic settings. You will find that, depending on your image, the default settings are not always the best ones to use.

2. On the same images, use the manual scanner controls at values other than default and automatic settings and compare your results. Perform one adjustment or function at a time to learn the effect of each tool.

3. Check the color values of your scan tests. For each scan test, open the image in Adobe Photoshop to determine whether enough scanning detail has been captured (see also "Evaluating a Scanned Image," page 24).

4. Output film from your tests and have professional proofs made. These proofs provide tangible information that will help you operate your scanner with consistent results.

Evaluating Image Characteristics

In addition to determining the correct scan resolution (see page 19), decide whether you want to match, enhance, or change the image for final reproduction. You might be able to accomplish some of these goals at the scanning stage. Consider the following questions while examining the images you plan to scan:

Focus. Are the main subject areas in focus? This is especially important if you plan to enlarge the image.

Color density. Are the colors vivid and fully saturated?

Color balance. Select an item in the image whose color you know, such as an orange or grass or snow. Is the color in your image true to the real thing?

Color cast. Does the overall color in your image shift, say, to green or blue? Some photographic films, shot under certain conditions, will produce a distinct color cast.

Graininess. Is the photograph grainy? If so, the graininess will probably become more apparent if you enlarge it. Certain films have more noticeable graininess than others; in general, prints tend to be grainier than transparencies.

Contrast. Examine the highlight and shadow detail areas carefully. Are the highlight areas "blown out" to flat white so that you can't see any detail? Are the shadow areas so dense they appear to be solid black? (See Chapter 3, "Color-Correcting and Editing Images.")

Imperfections. Are there obvious flaws in the image such as dust or scratches? The new Dust and Scratch filter in Photoshop 3.0 can eliminate these imperfections to some degree (see Chapter 3, "Color-Correcting and Editing Images," and the user guide for details).

Determining Scan Resolution

Whether you purchase a scan or do the scanning yourself, capturing the correct amount of image information is critical if you expect good final output. The optimal image (or scan) resolution depends on the halftone screen (in lpi) you need for printing, the file size (at times), and the dimensions of the final image. Too little pixel information may produce a fuzzy image, while capturing too many pixels will not improve the quality of your image if your output device is unable to use the extra pixel information. Excess resolution also increases the file size, which adds to the imaging time during scanning and makes the file more difficult to store, transfer, and edit.

Determining halftone screen. The appropriate halftone screen for printing is determined by three things: output quality, paper, and printing press. Higher halftone screen resolutions can provide more detail on press and are often used in high-quality printing such as art books and certain marketing brochures. You must also consider the paper selected for the job. High-quality coated papers enhance printing at higher halftone screen resolutions, but the same job at the same resolution printed on an uncoated, recycled stock might look muddy. Finally, printing presses often run best at certain halftone screens. Discuss these issues with your printer before choosing the halftone screen for your job, then use this information in determining the scan resolution (see "The Resolution Ratio," page 20).

Determining file size. Although some designers and production artists never consider file size when determining scan resolution, there are times when knowing this information early on could be useful. If, for instance, you are working with limited computer memory, you may need to keep your files as small as possible. Or if you are working on a document with many images on the same page or spread, small file sizes may facilitate your work. Without sacrificing quality, you may be able to scan images at lower resolutions to keep file sizes small (use the charts on page 22 as a guide). If file size is a determining factor in choosing your scan resolution, follow these steps:

1. Open Adobe Photoshop and choose New from the File menu. The New dialog box is used to calculate file size. Set the width and height measures to inches; set the resolution measure to pixels/inch; and choose Grayscale, RGB, or CMYK mode, as appropriate for your job.

2. When you fill in the Width, Height, and Resolution text boxes, Photoshop calculates the file size (Image Size) automatically. The resulting number is the file size; use this in your scanner's control panel.

Altering final image size. Typically, images aren't reproduced at their original sizes. For instance, if your original is a 35mm slide, chances are the image you reproduce will be larger when you go to press. Remember, though, that the image resolution you used for scanning is not automatically maintained when you alter the image's final output size. For example, a 1″ × 1″ image, scanned at 300 ppi, has 300 pixels in each direction. The same image resized to 2″ × 2″ (without changing the image resolution) has the same number of pixels in each direction (300), but the resolution changes to 150 ppi because those 300 pixels are now spread out over 2″.

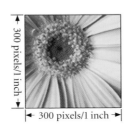 

300 pixels/1 inch | 150 pixels/1 inch | 150 pixels/1 inch

Consequently, scan resolution is determined by the final output size, not the size of the original. This is especially important if the output size is larger than the original.

If you are unsure of the final output size of your image, scan your image at a slightly higher resolution than you think you'll need so you'll have enough data in case you need to resize later.

The Resolution Ratio

The standard rule of thumb says that image (or scan) resolution should be twice the lines per inch of the halftone screen selected for printing (see "Determining Halftone Screen," page 19). But this isn't always true. Instead, the subject matter of your image should determine the correct scan resolution. The examples on these pages show several images reproduced at different ppi:lpi ratios. Examine them carefully. You'll see that the 2:1 ratio is not necessarily the best. The file sizes are also indicated so you can compare how the file size changes with different resolution ratios. The halftone screen for all images is 150 lpi.

The charts on page 22 show sample file sizes of images output at various dimensions and resolution ratios.

RATIO: 1:1   PPI: 150   SIZE: 606KB

RATIO: 1.5:1   PPI: 225   SIZE: 1.33MB

RATIO: 2:1   PPI: 300   SIZE: 2.36MB

RATIO: 3:1   PPI: 450   SIZE: 5.32MB

When purchasing color separations, always discuss the scanner's capabilities and your expectations of image quality with the vendor before the work begins. Also ask the vendor whether a for-position-only, low-resolution file and a color proof are included in the fee. High-end prepress vendors typically include these services, but not all do.

RGB FILE SIZE (150-LPI HALFTONE SCREEN)

OUTPUT SIZE	2:1 RESOLUTION RATIO							
	1″	2″	3″	4″	5″	6″	7″	8″
1″	264K / 149K	528K	792K	1.03M	1.29M	1.55M	1.80M	2.06M
2″	297K	1.03M / 594K	1.55M	2.06M	2.58M	3.09M	3.61M	4.12M
3″	445K	890K	2.32M / 1.30M	3.09M	3.86M	4.64M	5.41M	6.18M
4″	594K	1.16M	1.74M	4.12M / 2.32M	5.15M	6.18M	7.21M	8.24M
5″	742K	1.45M	2.17M	2.90M	6.44M / 3.62M	7.73M	9.01M	10.30M
6″	890K	1.74M	2.61M	3.48M	4.35M	9.27M / 5.21M	10.80M	12.40M
7″	1.01M	2.03M	3.04M	4.06M	5.07M	6.08M	12.6M / 7.10M	14.40M
8″	1.16M	2.32M	3.48M	4.64M	5.79M	6.95M	8.11M	16.5M / 9.27M

1.5:1 RESOLUTION RATIO

RGB FILE SIZE (175-LPI HALFTONE SCREEN)

OUTPUT SIZE	2:1 RESOLUTION RATIO							
	1″	2″	3″	4″	5″	6″	7″	8″
1″	359K / 203K	718K	1.05M	1.40M	1.75M	2.10M	2.45M	2.80M
2″	405K	1.40M / 808K	2.10M	2.80M	3.50M	4.21M	4.91M	5.61M
3″	608K	1.18M	3.15M / 1.78M	4.21M	5.26M	6.31M	7.36M	8.41M
4″	810K	1.58M	2.37M	5.61M / 3.15M	7.01M	8.41M	9.81M	11.20M
5″	1.01M	1.97M	2.96M	3.95M	8.76M / 4.93M	10.50M	12.30M	14.00M
6″	1.19M	2.37M	3.55M	4.73M	5.92M	12.6M / 7.10M	14.70M	16.80M
7″	1.38M	2.76M	4.14M	5.52M	6.91M	8.28M	17.2M / 9.67M	19.60M
8″	1.58M	3.15M	4.74M	6.31M	7.89M	9.46M	11.00M	22.4M / 12.6M

1.5:1 RESOLUTION RATIO

Keep these charts handy as you make your decisions during the scanning stage.

Resizing and Resampling Images

In general, it is always best to capture the correct amount of pixel information, at the size you need, during the scanning stage. Later adjustments may introduce unwanted changes in your image. But since this isn't always possible, you can resize an image using the capabilities of Adobe Photoshop.

Altering the dimensions of an image without adjusting its resolution changes its appearance and quality because the number of pixels per inch remains constant, regardless of the image size. (See "Altering Final Image Size," page 19.)

Resampling

To retain an image's visual integrity while changing its dimensions, you must also change its resolution. Changing the number of pixels in an image—its resolution—is called *resampling*.

When resampling, keep in mind that file size is proportional to scan resolution. For instance, the file size of an image scanned at 200 ppi is four times greater than the same image with the same dimensions scanned at 100 ppi.

200-ppi scan resolution; 380KB file size　　*100-ppi scan resolution; 96KB file size*

Resampling down decreases resolution and deletes pixel information from the image. *Resampling up* increases resolution and creates new pixel information based on existing color values.

Resampling down and then resampling up deteriorates the quality of an image. This happens because once an image is resampled down, the original pixel information is lost and cannot be recaptured unless you rescan the image.

When you resample up, Adobe Photoshop attempts to reconstruct the original color using the existing color information. However, the resulting image is only an approximation of the original and will not be as sharp or as accurate.

Interpolation

Interpolation is the process by which Adobe Photoshop fills in or deletes pixels when an image is changed significantly. It occurs any time you rotate, scale, skew, change perspective in, or resample an image. Regardless of direction, resampling alters the color of some pixels during interpolation. When you resample up, you essentially create blank pixels. As the image size increases, new pixels are created to fill the blank pixels, based on the color values of surrounding pixels. When you resample down, certain pixels are deleted to make the image smaller, and some of the remaining pixel colors are changed to approximate the visual appearance of pixels that have been deleted. There are three methods of interpolation available in Photoshop: Bicubic, Nearest Neighbor, and Bilinear. Select one based on the output quality you'll need and the type of image you are interpolating.

Bicubic. This is the most precise form of interpolation because of its precise method of selecting pixels for emulation. The Bicubic method should be used whenever you need exacting quality. It is the most time-consuming interpolation method.

Nearest Neighbor. This is the fastest type of interpolation, but not especially subtle in the way it selects pixels to emulate. In most cases, the result is an image with a jagged appearance. Use Nearest Neighbor when you wish to preserve the crisp nature of line art or illustrations that use pixels as design elements; in most cases use Nearest Neighbor when resampling screen shots. (For screen shots, when possible resample down by dividing your original resolution by a whole number, not a decimal. For instance, if your original image was 600 ppi, the best result for resampling would occur at 75, 150, or 300 ppi.)

Bilinear. Bilinear interpolation reproduces pixel information in a manner similar to that of Bicubic, but does not provide the same level of detail enhancement; Bilinear also takes less time than Bicubic, but more time than Nearest Neighbor.

Continous-tone image

Enlarged section using Bicubic

Enlarged section using Nearest Neighbor

Grayscale image

Enlarged section using Bicubic

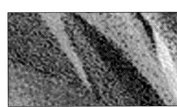

Enlarged section using Nearest Neighbor

Pixelated image

Enlarged section using Bicubic

Enlarged section using Nearest Neighbor

Apply Unsharp Mask to your image after resampling up, rotating, scaling, skewing, or changing perspectives to help refocus it.

Whenever you resample up, make sure your new file has enough image information to reproduce well at that size.

Using the Info Palette

You can use the Info palette to quickly determine whether you have captured adequate tonal range during scanning. First, open the image and the Info palette (Window/Show Info). Then use the eyedropper tool to measure values in the highlight and shadow regions of your scanned image. In general, highlights should measure between 240 and 250 in RGB mode and between 5% and 10% in CMYK mode. In most cases, shadows reproduce well at measures of between 5 and 10 in RGB and between 90% and 95% in CMYK. For more information about highlight and shadow values, see Chapter 3, "Color-Correcting and Editing Images."

Getting the Best Kodak Photo CD Image

Certain third-party products offer extra functionality beyond what comes with Adobe Photoshop. Using the Kodak Acquire module (version 2.01 for the Macintosh and version 1.0 for the Windows platform), for instance, you can quickly adjust the Gamma and color-temperature values of scans, which usually results in better tonal range than if you used the image as scanned. To do this:

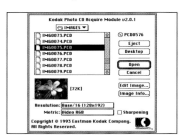

1. In Photoshop, choose Acquire/ Kodak Photo CD and select an image from the disc.

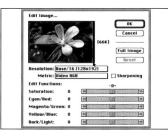

2. Click Edit Image to see a larger preview. Using the pointer tool, roughly crop the preview image by clicking in the upper left-hand corner and dragging the red box to the lower right-hand corner, making sure you crop out any black or white borders.

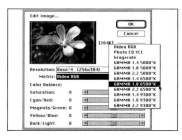

3. Select the Base/4 (256 × 384) version of the image. Select a Gamma setting and color temperature (a good place to start is 1.8 for Gamma and 6500° Kelvin for temperature). Click OK.

4. Open the image in Photoshop and evaluate it using a histogram (see the next section). To get more tonal range from the scan, try using different Gamma and temperature settings. Evaluate these test settings and write down the ones that give the best results.

5. Using the best Gamma and color-temperature settings determined in step 4, reopen the image at the resolution required for output. Your image is ready for further color correction in Photoshop if necessary.

Evaluating a Scanned Image

Before spending hours color-correcting or editing images for final reproduction, first evaluate the scans to determine whether adequate pixel information has been captured to achieve the results you want.

To do this, consider how the final image will be used: Should it match, enhance, or differ from the original? To match images to the originals for reproduction, the scanned images should duplicate the colors and detail as they appear in the original images. Enhancing a scanned image to look better than the original is often done to compensate for an inadequate original. For instance, the image might look flat because there isn't enough contrast, or there might be a color cast in the film. Editing or color-correcting an image so that it looks different from the original might be done to change the color of an object, to remove an item you don't want, or to add something you do want.

To evaluate a scan in Adobe Photoshop, examine the image and its histogram. A *histogram* is a graphic representation of the tonal range of pixels as gray values (or brightness levels) from 0 to 255. To select the histogram used for evaluation, open Image/Adjust/Levels; the Levels dialog box appears. You can view combined channels in RGB or CMYK mode. In RGB mode, the histogram displays the shadow region to the highlight region from left to right. Click the bar at the bottom of the graph to switch to CMYK percentages; in this mode, the percentage values read from light to dark, left to right. You can also examine individual channels by clicking on the Channel pop-up menu in the Levels dialog box and selecting a specific channel. By comparing histograms to the image, you can evaluate scans and determine whether adequate pixel data has been captured for reproduction.

Inadequate tonal range results in too little contrast overall; the scanned image looks flat.

The blue channel is too dense for this image compared with the green and red channels; this results in a blue color cast.

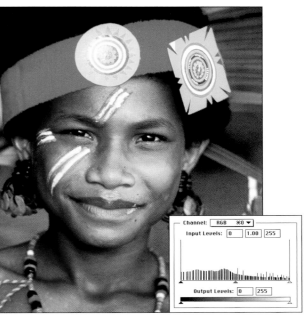

The scanner did not capture enough detail, which results in a "gappy" scan; the image should probably be rescanned.

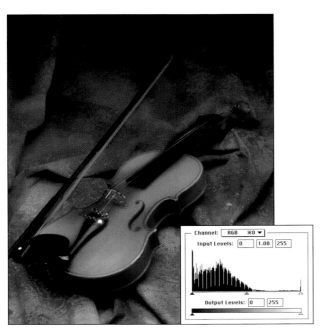

Pixel information is too dense in the shadow area; details in this region are lost.

The tonal values are weighted in the shadow region; pixels should be more evenly distributed throughout the histogram.

A lack of pixels in the brightest highlights results in a total loss of detail in this region.

Color-Correcting and Editing Images

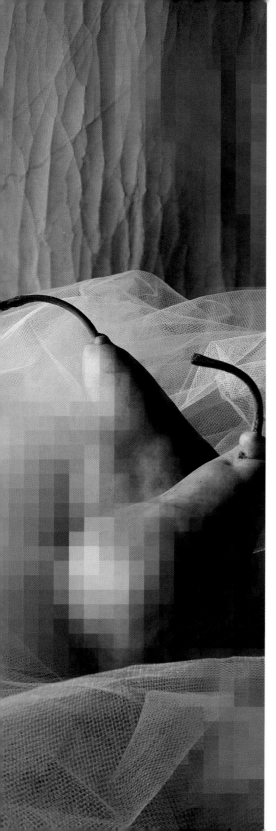

Color-Correcting and Editing Images

Matching, enhancing, and changing original images to reproduce as you like is a skill once left entirely to highly trained professionals. With Adobe Photoshop and a solid understanding of how it is designed to color-correct and edit images, you can do all or some of this work yourself.

This chapter offers various approaches for color-correcting and editing scanned images using the tools in Adobe Photoshop. Most of the image editing information you will find in this chapter applies to black-and-white as well as color reproduction. Unless otherwise specified, assume that these steps and techniques will work for either.

Why Correct Color?

Color correction is often necessary to reproduce color accurately on press. Reasons for this might be that the original has a color cast (possibly caused by using incorrect film or lighting during photography); the scan is imperfect (the scanner might introduce color casts or artifacts, for instance); or you cannot match your original art because of deficiencies in the printing process (impure printing inks can introduce muddiness). Whether you purchase scans or do them yourself, obtain the best scans possible to begin with—if detail does not exist in the scan, you can't add it later.

If using high-end scanned images, make sure you discuss your expectations with your prepress vendor before the scanning process begins. Most flaws in originals can be eliminated by a skilled scanner operator who knows what you want. Check color proofs of individual images before they are placed in a page layout document; this ensures good color reproduction early in the production process.

Using a Color-Correction Strategy

Good color reproduction results in printed images with a proper range of tones from light to dark that provide correct brightness and contrast, good hues and saturation, and balanced colors appropriate for the image's critical areas of interest. Performing color-correction tasks systematically helps you achieve the best results most efficiently.

Depending on the level of color correction an image requires, you may not need to perform certain steps described here, or you may change the order in which you do them. For example, after adjusting the highlights and shadows, you may not need to adjust the midtones; or you may adjust for a color cast before adjusting the midtones.

The tips and techniques in this chapter have been used by experts in the field but are not the only ways to approach color correction and image editing. For more ideas, see the *Adobe Photoshop 3.0 Tutorial.*

COLOR-CORRECTION STRATEGY

1. Make sure your system is calibrated and that your preferences are set for your printing environment before you begin (see "Calibrating Your System" in Chapter 1 and Chapter 6, "Preparing and Printing Files").

2. Acquire and open the image in Adobe Photoshop (see Chapter 2, "Acquiring Images").

3. Evaluate the scanned image (see "Evaluating a Scanned Image" in Chapter 2) and decide which color mode to work in (page 29).

4. Make a copy of the original scan and resize if necessary.

5. Identify the image key type (page 30).

6. Adjust for good tone reproduction (page 32).

7. Apply color-correction tools as necessary.

8. Sharpen the image (page 41).

9. Convert the RGB image to CMYK if it is not already a CMYK file (page 49).

10. If necessary, fine-tune the image in CMYK mode (page 49).

Choosing the Right Color Mode

Differences exist between RGB and CMYK modes that might make you wonder which mode is best. There are a variety of reasons for working in either mode—ultimately, you should decide for yourself based on the images you work with, your experience, your system, and your goals for printing on paper. (To better understand why differences exist and how they affect color correction and image editing, see "Basic Concepts" in the *Adobe Photoshop 3.0 User Guide.*)

RGB Mode

Typical desktop scans are in RGB mode and will probably require some color correction. Many experts believe it is best to do corrections and editing in RGB mode before converting to CMYK, for the following reasons:

RGB files are smaller than CMYK files. Because there are only three channels of information in RGB files, rather than four as in CMYK, RGB files are smaller. Overall, work is usually faster in RGB.

You can adjust out-of-gamut colors in RGB mode. In RGB mode, Adobe Photoshop 3.0 will find, identify, and let you adjust *out-of-gamut colors;* that is, colors that display on the monitor but cannot be printed in CMYK. If you separate an image with out-of-gamut colors without adjusting them, Photoshop adjusts them automatically.

Some tools and functions perform better in RGB mode. Because of the way Adobe Photoshop is engineered, certain color-correction functions (Hue/Saturation, for instance) are more accurate in RGB mode than in CMYK mode.

You can alter the printing preferences of color-corrected RGB files. If you perform color corrections in CMYK mode, you can't alter the Printing Inks Setup or Separation Setup settings selected in Preferences without converting (or reverting) to RGB, then reconverting back to CMYK. This is important if the same image needs to be reproduced in several printing environments. For instance, the image might appear in a newspaper ad, a high-quality brochure, and a poster printed using European-standard inks. By working in RGB mode, you can create, load, and save a variety of Preferences settings. Converting back and forth can result in poor image quality and some color loss.

CMYK Mode

If you have communicated well with your prepress vendor, high-end CMYK scans shouldn't need much correction (see Chapter 2, "Acquiring Images"). If they do, you should continue to work in CMYK mode when possible. If you have an RGB scan, however, should you convert to CMYK before making corrections? Occasionally you might want to; consider the following points when deciding:

Work in CMYK mode if your system is not calibrated. If you haven't calibrated your system, the only way to color-correct is in CMYK mode using numerical values in the Info palette. In general, it is best to calibrate your system (see "Calibrating Your System" in Chapter 1).

You can match halftone-dot percentages precisely in CMYK mode. If you are working in RGB, the CMYK readout in the Info palette is sufficiently accurate in most cases. But if you need to specify very dark, saturated colors, you can do this more precisely in CMYK mode.

Work in CMYK mode if you need to edit existing CMYK images. If a particular job requires editing, such as changing the color of red wine to white, it doesn't make sense to convert to RGB to make corrections and then reconvert to CMYK. If you do, you might change some of your original pixel data.

You can produce better gradients in CMYK mode. To produce gradients for printed work in Adobe Photoshop, create them in the final output mode, which is CMYK—the results are much smoother than when you create them in RGB mode.

Why Is Neutrality Important?

In general, people have expectations about how colors should appear. Most of us know sky blue, green grass, flesh tones, and neutral whites, grays, or blacks, for instance. This concept of preconceived "memory" colors is the basis for understanding color balance and neutrality. When colors are skewed or biased from what we expect, strange shifts known as *color casts* occur that throw off the whole image. The results are visually disturbing. When neutral areas in an image actually appear neutral, the rest of the image usually looks balanced. Therefore, maintaining balance in neutrals throughout the reproduction process is critical for good results on press.

Experts often separate colors into *hues*—actual colors such as red, blue, or yellow—and *gray,* which includes tones between white and black that have no color. *Gray balance* refers to the combination of colors (CMY or RGB) that produces neutral gray. Understanding gray

Each time you click OK in a color-adjustment dialog box, Adobe Photoshop adjusts pixels using complex mathematical equations, and the color data in your file is permanently altered. Thus, your goal during correction and editing should be to perform as few adjustments as you need to achieve the results you want. Overediting and overcorrection may result in a degradation of pixel values.

Before producing a gradient in Adobe Photoshop, be sure to select Smoother under CMYK Composites in General Preferences and check the Dither box within the Gradient Tool Options palette.

Finding the Hidden Grayscale

If you don't scan a grayscale strip with your original image, it is sometimes difficult to find a neutral gray within it. Finding the neutral gray in an image helps you establish neutrality so you can balance the colors in that image overall. By examining the image closely in the highlight, quarter-tone, midtone, three-quarter-tone, and shadow areas that you know, or might guess, should be neutral, you can find the hidden grayscale. For instance, asphalt paving, automobile tires, the shadows in a white shirt, the deep folds in clothing, a gray computer, or deep shadows cast by an object might contain neutral gray. By ensuring that these areas are made neutral, using various techniques described in this chapter, you may find that the color balance in the rest of your image falls in line.

balance is important because the relationship of the amounts of printing inks used to reproduce a balanced gray also affects the way colors are reproduced on press.

Equal amounts of RGB produce neutral gray; therefore, you might guess that equal amounts of CMY do, too. But they don't. The reason is that the pigments used to make printing inks are contaminated. Cyan ink contains a lot of magenta and even some yellow, and magenta ink also contains yellow and a little cyan. To compensate for this, different combinations of CMY inks are needed to make balanced colors. To further complicate matters, different combinations of CMY are used to produce balanced grays and neutral colors, depending on a particular printing environment and on where the neutrals exist in the range of tones from highlights to shadows.

The following chart compares neutral gray RGB values with CMY values that could be used to produce an average image on coated stock (see Chapter 6, "Preparing and Printing Files"). Notice the differences, especially in the midtone region, between the cyan ink percentage and the yellow and magenta percentages. To maintain neutrality, this differential relationship among the printing inks must be maintained throughout the reproduction process. In Adobe Photoshop, this relationship is built into the separation tables and is interpreted when you convert from RGB mode to CMYK mode.

TYPICAL NEUTRAL VALUES						
	R	G	B	C	M	Y
	DIGITAL VALUES			PERCENT VALUES		
PAPER WHITE	255	255	255	0%	0%	0%
HIGHLIGHT	250	250	250	5%	3%	3%
¼ TONE	190	190	190	28%	21%	21%
MIDTONE	128	128	128	62%	50%	50%
¾ TONE	68	68	68	78%	66%	66%
SHADOW	5	5	5	95%	85%	85%
EXTREME BLACK POINT	0	0	0	100%	89%	85%

Equivalent RGB and CMY ink values used to produce neutral gray

Unfortunately, neutrality can be compromised at every step of the reproduction process.

- During photography, improper lighting and film combinations often cause color casts in film.

- Scanners can introduce color casts because their technology might interpret colors differently than we see them or because the scanner operator adjusts the scanner incorrectly.

- If you open an image on a monitor that is not calibrated to neutral gray, your color adjustments, although accurate on-screen, may introduce disturbing color casts when printed.

- If your monitor is calibrated but you haven't set the preferences appropriately for your printing conditions, you will still have trouble maintaining good neutrals and balanced color on press. This is because the separation table that defines the translation of RGB values to CMYK values will be off.

- Color shifts can occur on press because combining ink, water, and oil at very high speeds and transferring them to paper is an art form in itself, requiring experience to do well.

Identifying Key Type

The term *key type* is used to define the regions in an image that are, or should be, the most compelling. Identifying the key type of an image helps you pinpoint detail areas where corrections should be focused (see "Tone Compression," page 32).

High key images tend to be light overall and have pixels concentrated in the highlight region—the area ranging from the highlights to the midtones. *Average key* images concentrate pixels in the midtone region. *Low key* images concentrate details in the shadow region (which ranges from midtone to shadows) and tend to be dark.

For the best printed results, make corrections where it counts. For instance, consider what makes a particular image most captivating— is it the highlight region, the shadow details, or the midtones? A high key image whose focus is in the highlight region should be corrected to enhance the highlight details. The shadow areas in such an image may go flat as a result, but this effect will hardly be noticed.

HIGH KEY

AVERAGE KEY

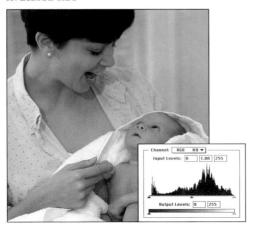

LOW KEY

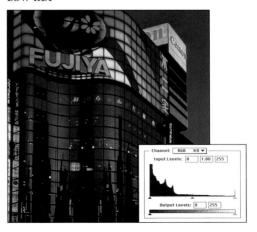

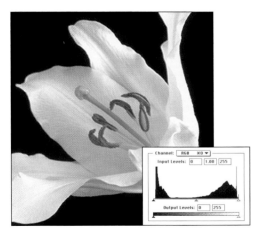

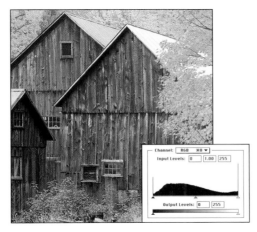

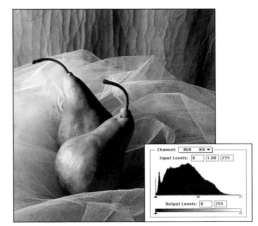

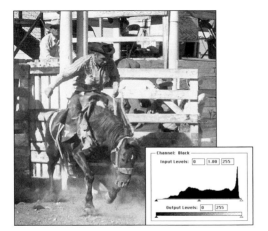

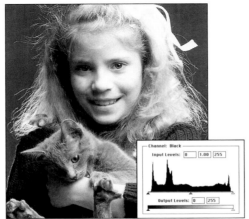

Reading a Histogram

Some images are not obviously high, average, or low key. By looking at the histogram of an image, you can isolate where the pixels are concentrated to help identify its key type (choose Image/Adjust/Levels to view an image's histogram). See "Evaluating a Scanned Image" in Chapter 2 and the *Adobe Photoshop User Guide* for more information about histograms.

In RGB mode, a histogram that shows a concentration of pixels to the right denotes a high key image; one that shows pixels concentrated in the middle indicates an average image; and one with pixels concentrated to the left indicates a low key image. Sometimes an image has a concentration of pixels at both ends. In this case, based on the subject of the image, you'll need to determine exactly where you want the focus of interest to be.

Tone Compression

The key to good reproduction is optimizing the number of tonal values available for printing as compared to what you can see on-screen. During each phase of reproduction – photography, scanning, color correction, separation, outputting film, making printing plates, and finally printing the image onto paper – the range of tones available is reduced or compressed. You can control this compression to some degree by adjusting the tonal range of an image so that the highlights are bright and neutral, the midtones aren't muddy or clogged, and the shadows, while dark and saturated, maintain detail.

Depending on the key type of your image, you can choose where to utilize the pixel values captured during scanning so that your particular image will reproduce well in a given set of printing conditions.

Adjusting for Good Tone Reproduction

Good tone reproduction is evident in images with contrast adjustments focused on important details; balanced neutrals; and clean, bright colors throughout. By adjusting the highlight, shadow, and midtone regions of images, you can enhance details in these key areas, establish neutrality, and achieve good tone reproduction.

This section explains how to define the range of pixels that will give you the best tone reproduction for a particular image. The tonal adjustments in the following techniques have been applied to RGB images (see also "Choosing the Right Color Mode," page 29). If your image is a good CMYK scan, you probably will not need to make all the adjustments described here. At the end of this section, several images are shown that have been color-corrected starting with setting end points, through fine-tuning in CMYK (see pages 36-37). Examine these images carefully to help you make color-correction decisions.

Determining End Points

Compressing or widening the tonal range of pixels available in a scan often improves the quality of the image. To do this, you assign end points (also known as setting the white and black points) that define or map the tonal range of pixels from the extreme highlight (*white point*) to the extreme shadow (*black point*), thus achieving a printable highlight and a printable shadow. Note that some images—a close-up of roses that fill the image area, for instance—might not have a true white or black; when setting the end points for such an image, try to achieve a range of brightness from highlight to shadow that will print with appropriate contrast and "punch."

Original image   *Adjusted for brightness*

A *printable highlight,* sometimes known as the *diffuse highlight,* is the region in the tonal range of an image that contains the lightest details that print; the image areas beyond the white point are known as *specular highlights* and are sometimes referred to as *paper white.* When selecting a white point, try to find an area that contains some tonal

value. If you choose an area to set the white point that contains too much tone, the image could become too light or appear "blown out" because all highlights beyond the white point become paper white.

A *printable shadow* is the portion of the tonal range that contains the darkest details that print; the areas beyond the black point are solid black. If the black point you choose is too light, the image gets darker overall and the contrast increases inappropriately.

Correct settings for end points   *Incorrect settings for end points*

Determining Target Values

Most images used in print production need to be free of color casts and maintain neutrality to reproduce accurately. To achieve this, you can determine the correct highlight and shadow target values for your image and printing conditions. *Target values* are predetermined printing ink settings used to define and neutralize end points. These values are designed to neutralize slight color casts in images overall. Distinct color casts usually require more color correction (see "Adjusting Color Balance," page 38).

To determine correct target values for your particular printing environment, start by talking to your printer. Your printer can specify neutral end-point values for the paper, ink, and printing press you'll be using. Use the numbers your printer provides when you set the white and black points. If your printer cannot provide these values, you can either produce a CMY neutrals chart that will help you establish precise values for your particular reproduction system (see Chapter 6, "Preparing and Printing Files") or use target values based on standard printing environments and the separation tables built into Photoshop.

The highlight target values used most often with Adobe Photoshop are Cyan: 5%, Magenta: 3%, Yellow: 3%, and Black: 0%; the shadow target values are Cyan: 65%, Magenta: 53%, Yellow: 51%, and Black: 95%. These are merely target values, however. Depending on your image, you might find that altering these values slightly will give you better results (see also the *Adobe Photoshop 3.0 Tutorial*).

Setting End Points to Target Values

To set the white point for the highlights, assign target CMY values to that end point. Doing this defines ink values for printing that give you neutral highlights.

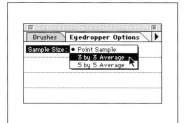

1. Open your image and the Info palette (Window/Palettes/Show Info). Double-click on the eyedropper tool to open the Eyedropper Options palette, and make sure the Sample Size is set to 3 by 3 Average.

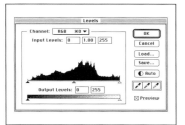

2. Choose Image/Adjust/Levels; the Levels dialog box appears. The histogram shown here indicates an average key image. Check the Preview box so you can view the results of your changes.

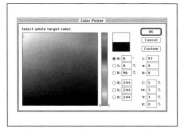

3. Double-click on the white eyedropper in the Levels dialog box to display the Color Picker. Enter the highlight target values (C: 5, M: 3, Y: 3, and K: 0); click OK.

4. In the Info palette, check the values while moving the white eyedropper around the image to find the white point (this is the lightest printable highlight). Try several spots; a white point that contains detail isn't always apparent (we chose the cuff on the man's shirt). To set the highlight target values, click the area you identified as the white point with the eyedropper.

5. Double-click on the black eyedropper in the Levels dialog box; the Color Picker appears. Enter the shadow target values (we used C: 65, M: 53, Y: 51, and K: 95). Click OK. Check Info palette values as you move the eyedropper around the image to find the black point.

6. To set the shadow target values, click the area you identified as the black point with the eyedropper.

Setting End Points for Certain Paper Types

If your project is printing on newsprint, recycled stock, or colored paper, the end points might need to be set differently than if printing on a coated premium paper. Under such conditions, you might need to set the white point so that the image has more specular highlights and less solid black than normal. The reason for this is that newsprint, recycled stock, and colored papers are darker and usually more absorbent than a pure white coated sheet. Therefore, these papers don't always provide enough contrast between the paper, the lightest highlights, and the darkest shadows. Absorbency is a concern on these papers because dot gain is greater than it is on coated stock (see Chapter 6, "Preparing and Printing Files"). Setting the end points so that you have the correct amounts of specular highlights and solid black areas improves contrast overall and allows for dot gain. Because images vary greatly, determining end points to adjust the specular highlights and solid black areas precisely is very image-dependent. Over time, experience will help you choose the right settings.

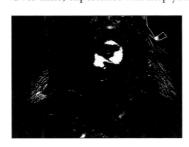

1. Open your image. Choose Image/Adjust/Levels; the Levels dialog box appears. Make sure the Preview box is unchecked. While holding down the Option key, move the white Input triangle to the left; the first white areas you see are the brightest highlights.

Finding End Points Using Levels

To find the lightest highlights in an image, open the Levels dialog box. Hold down the Option key while dragging the right Input triangle slowly toward the left (make sure the Preview box is unchecked). The first areas that appear white are the brightest areas in the image. Unless you want to set your white point, either return the triangle to its original position or click the Cancel button.

To find the shadows, use Levels as you did for the highlights, this time dragging the left Input triangle to the right. The first black areas you see are the darkest shadows in the image. Unless you want to set your black point, either return the slider to its original position or click the Cancel button.

If you have trouble previewing and have a 24- or 32-bit video card, certain color QuickDraw commands may have been implemented improperly in your card. Contact your video card manufacturer for ROM updates.

To better control your curve adjustments, especially if you are new to Curves, drag the point on the curve that you want to adjust straight up or straight down, using the grid in the background as a guide. This focuses the impact of the curve adjustment on the point selected, although it also affects the rest of the curve unless you anchor points on either side of your adjustment.

2. As you continue to move the triangle to the left, more areas turn white, thus increasing the specular highlight region. When you reach the correct white point for your image, release both the Option key and the triangle.

3. To set the black point, move the black Input triangle slowly to the right while holding down the Option key; the first black areas you see are the darkest shadows. Release the Option key and the triangle when you reach the correct black point.

4. With the end points set for your image, click OK in the Levels dialog box. Here, we have simulated what the image would look like on a slightly colored, absorbent stock such as newsprint.

Setting End Points for Images with Narrow Tonal Range

Although not as precise as assigning target values, you can also use the Input Levels triangles (in the Levels dialog box) to set end points for images when you identify a narrow tonal range in the histogram. Use this method when neutralizing the image is not a factor. If your image does not contain enough tonal range to begin with, however, this approach may make your image look worse because it spreads the existing pixels over a broader tonal range.

1. Open your image and choose Image/Adjust/Levels. In the Levels dialog box, check the Preview box. To set the white point, move the right Input triangle to the point in the histogram where the highlight values begin.

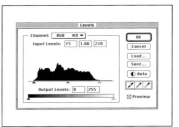

2. To set the black point, move the black Input triangle to the point in the histogram where the shadows begin. (To achieve more contrast, try moving the triangles just inside both ends of the histogram.)

3. With the end points set, click OK in the Levels dialog box. In this image, adjusting the end points of the histogram brightened the image overall and added a bit of contrast.

Adjusting Midtones

Making adjustments in the midtone areas of an image can improve image quality dramatically by enhancing the contrast and adjusting brightness in important detail areas. For instance, to enhance detail in the highlight areas of an image, darken the midtones; this results in shadow areas with less contrast. Conversely, you can enhance the detail in the shadow areas by lightening the midtones; this results in highlights with less detail. You may not need to make any midtone adjustments in some images; average key images often require no more tonal adjustments than setting the white and black points. In the following examples, we show two midtone curve adjustments; each results in the correct adjustment for that particular image.

Simple Curve Adjustment

1. With your image open, choose Image/Adjust/Curves; the Curves dialog box appears. Check the Preview box and set Curves to percentage mode. Examine your image for brightness and contrast.

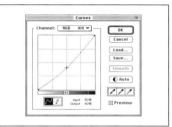

2. With the pointer at the mid-point junction, adjust the curve by dragging it down to increase brightness or dragging it up to darken the image.

3. Adjust the curve until a point is found that gives the desired contrast and brightness; click OK.

Anchored Curve Adjustment

1. With your image open, choose Image/Adjust/Curves; the Curves dialog box appears. Check the Preview box and set Curves to percentage mode. Examine your image for brightness and contrast.

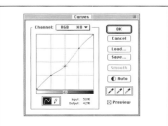

2. Place anchor points at the one-quarter and three-quarter junctions on the curve by clicking on those points. With the pointer at the midpoint, adjust the curve by dragging it down to brighten the image or by dragging it up to darken the image.

3. When you find the point that gives the desired contrast and brightness, click OK.

Fine-Tuning Midtones Using Curves

Adjusting the quarter and three-quarter tones in an image lets you adjust details in specific image regions while maintaining details in other areas.

You can do this by adjusting the quarter tones using Curves. One of the more common tonal adjustments results in an S-curve. This curve adjustment produces an image with higher contrast—the midtones gain detail and the transition between highlights and shadows is more dramatic, giving the resulting image more "snap."

BEFORE   **AFTER**

S-curve adjustment

Quarter-tone adjustment

Adjusting Curves

Make highlight, shadow, and midtone adjustments using either Levels or Curves. Curves give you more precise control, though, since you can make adjustments at sixteen points along the curve rather than just the highlight, shadow, and midtone regions that you can adjust in the Levels dialog box.

Anchoring points on a curve helps you isolate adjustments to specific tonal areas. You may want to anchor the quarter and three-quarter points to adjust the midpoint. To anchor a point on a curve, simply click the place on the curve that you want to remain fixed. To remove an anchor point, simply drag it off the grid.

Make sure the Curves dialog box is set to the mode you're working in. The graph reads in levels of gray or brightness values (0–255) when the gradation bar at the bottom indicates that the shadows are on the left and the highlights are on the right. Or you can toggle to percentage mode (0%–100%) by clicking on the bar.

Original RGB image: low contrast overall

Set black and white points

Adjusted Curves to lighten mid- to three-quarter tones

Converted to CMYK; applied Unsharp Mask and Selective Color

Original RGB image: overall yellow color cast

Set black and white points

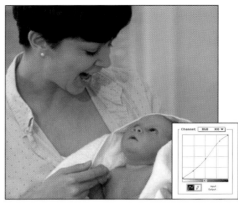

Adjusted Curves to remove cast from woman's face and neck

Converted to CMYK; applied Unsharp Mask

Original RGB image: lacks contrast in midtones

Set black and white points

Adjusted Curves to lighten three-quarter and darken quarter tones

Converted to CMYK; applied Unsharp Mask

Original RGB image: lacks detail in three-quarter-tone region

Set black and white points

Adjusted Curves to darken midtones and lighten three-quarter and quarter tones

Converted to CMYK; applied Unsharp Mask

Original RGB image: too dark; shadows need to be "opened up" or brightened

Set black and white points

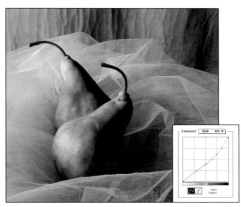

Adjusted Curves to brighten image overall

Converted to CMYK; applied Unsharp Mask and Selective Color

Black-on-black grayscale image: needs more contrast in shadow region to distinguish tones

Set black and white points

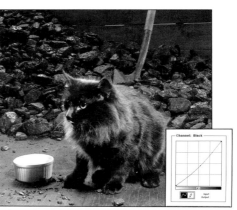

Adjusted Curves at midpoint to enhance contrast

Applied Unsharp Mask

Determining End Points Using Curves

You can identify the black and white points in an image using Curves. Open your image and the Curves dialog box. Move the eyedropper around the image while holding down the mouse button and watch the circle on the curve. When the circle is closest to the highlight end of the curve and the density is low, you've found the lightest area in the image; use this to determine the white point. To find the darkest area of the image and to isolate the black point, repeat the process in reverse (the circle is closest to the shadow end of the curve and the density is high).

Adjusting Color Balance

After setting end points and adjusting midtones, examine your image further to determine whether your image has a color balance problem. If a color cast exists—if skin tones seem greenish, for instance, or a neutral area shows a distinct color (see "Why Is Neutrality Important?" on page 29)—you'll need to adjust the color balance.

Bracketing Photographic Images

Improper color balance is often attributable to imbalances among the color layers of photographic film and improper lighting. Imbalances in film are similar to the variances produced by bracketed exposures.

Photographic film is made up of three layers—cyan, magenta, and yellow, the yellow layer being sandwiched between the cyan and magenta (you can see this for yourself if you slice a piece of film with an X-Acto knife). You can also think of color photographic film as being made up of three grayscale layers, each of which could have a normal exposure or be overexposed or underexposed. In a perfect world, these three layers would each have a normal exposure and thus produce perfectly balanced color. Despite the best efforts of film manufacturers, however, this is rarely the case. Instead, at least one layer of the film is usually over- or underexposed, causing a color cast that affects the overall neutrality of the image.

By shooting the same scene multiple times with different lens-aperture settings, shutter speeds, and/or filters, a photographer can control how an image is captured on film and compensate, to some degree, for the imbalances among layers of film. This is called *bracketing* and it is done to ensure that the correct and best exposure for the scene has been captured for reproduction. You can utilize the concept of bracketing to help evaluate and correct color casts in specific channels of RGB or CMYK scanned images.

Normal exposure *Overexposure* *Underexposure*

Balancing Bracketed Exposures

In the following example, we examine a bracketed grayscale image and then, using Curves in Adobe Photoshop, balance the overexposure and underexposure to the normal exposure. This approach will help you gain a better understanding of how to identify and adjust color casts in color images.

Normal exposure

Overexposure

Underexposure

Notice the signs of over- and underexposure in this example as compared to the normal exposure. The overexposed image appears lighter overall and has little contrast or detail in the highlight areas. The underexposed image, which is darker overall, has too much detail in the highlights and very little in the shadows.

Using the Info palette and the eyedropper tool, we examine tonal values in the highlight and shadow regions of each exposure. In the overexposed image, the percentage values are lower in the highlights and shadows than they are in the normal exposure (see the chart below). In the underexposed image, the opposite is true—both the shadows and the highlights are too dense.

COMPARISON OF WHITE AND BLACK POINTS		
	HIGHLIGHT	SHADOW
NORMAL EXPOSURE	5	95
OVEREXPOSURE	1	88
UNDEREXPOSURE	18	98

Overexposure after adjustment

Underexposure after adjustment

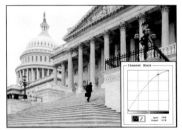

Overexposure after adjustment

Underexposure after adjustment

When the highlight and shadow values in the over- and under-exposed images are adjusted to match the values in the normal exposure, notice how the two exposures become more like the normal exposure.

Finally, by adjusting the over- and underexposed images in the quarter, mid-, and three-quarter tones using Curves, they nearly match the normal exposure. Also notice the differences in the Curves dialog box for each exposure after these adjustments are made.

Using Curves to Balance Color Casts

To adjust imbalanced color channels that produce color casts, look for areas in your image that you expect to be neutral but are not. Then identify which channels are exposed incorrectly, thus creating the color cast. Correct the cast by "normalizing" the badly exposed channels using Curves. After correcting the color cast, continue to make color corrections as necessary. There are many ways to eliminate color casts; this example uses Curves (see the *Adobe Photoshop 3.0 Tutorial* for more ideas on how to correct color balance).

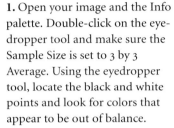

1. Open your image and the Info palette. Double-click on the eye-dropper tool and make sure the Sample Size is set to 3 by 3 Average. Using the eyedropper tool, locate the black and white points and look for colors that appear to be out of balance.

2. In the General Preferences dialog box, leave the Color Channels in Color box unchecked. Click on each channel in the Channels palette and examine it in grayscale.

In this example, the Red channel is overexposed, the Green channel appears normal, and the Blue channel is underexposed.

Choose Window/New Window to open a second version of your original image; use it to preview your image in color as you make adjustments to the individual channels in grayscale. (Zoom it down to a smaller size and move it to the side so you can see the channel you're working on.) After adjusting the preview window, highlight the window of your original image.

Adjusting a Single Channel

You can use Curves to pinpoint obvious color casts and correct them easily. With the Info palette and the Curves dialog box open, determine which channel might have the color cast. In the Curves dialog box, select the suspect channel in the Channel pop-up menu. Using the plain eyedropper, find a neutral area. While holding down the mouse button, place the eyedropper on the neutral area and notice its values in the Info palette to verify that it has a color cast. Also notice where this area falls on the curve; by adjusting that point on the curve, you can correct the color cast. You may need to anchor the points around this area on the curve to isolate your correction.

You can set tonal range, adjust contrast, and balance color using just Curves. It requires a careful eye, experience with Curves, and an idea of what you expect of the outcome. Once you are comfortable using Curves, you can make all your tonal adjustments in this one dialog box. The cat image on this page shows that contrast and end points are adjusted first in the normal (Red) channel; you then adjust the other channels to approximate this one.

3. View the normal channel (Green in this example) by clicking on it in the Channels palette. Using the eyedropper tool, determine the values of the white and black points located in step 1 (5% and 95% in our example).

4. Select the overexposed channel (Red in this example). Choose Curves, make sure the Preview box is checked, and set Curves to percentage mode. To darken the image, drag the lower left-hand corner up to the white point value determined in step 3 (5%).

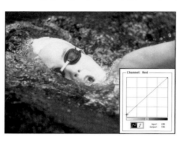

5. Move the upper right-hand corner of the curve down to the shadow value (95%). Adjust the quarter, mid-, and three-quarter tones to "normalize" the channel. Watch the color window as you work; be careful not to introduce too much contrast. Click OK.

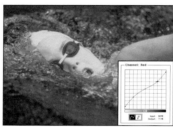

6. Select the underexposed channel (Blue in this example). Choose Curves and set the end points of the curve to the white and black points (5% and 95%), as in steps 4 and 5.

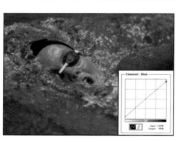

7. To normalize the Blue channel, adjust the curve in the midtone region to lighten the image, then click OK.

8. Once satisfied with the adjustments you have made, click on the RGB composite in the Channels palette and close the preview window. The image is now ready for any further color correction.

RGB original with a color cast   *RGB image with color adjusted*

Red channel (normal exposure)   *Red channel after adjustment*

Green channel (overexposure)   *Green channel after adjustment*

Blue channel (underexposure)   *Blue channel after adjustment*

Using Unsharp Masking

In traditional color reproduction, color separations are made photo-graphically and masks are applied to the layers of film as they are shot to enhance the contrast between neighboring areas of color. This process is called *unsharp masking*. High-contrast edges are exaggerated throughout an image when unsharp masking is applied. This gives an image more contrast in these areas and enriches detail overall.

The amount of unsharp masking you apply using Adobe Photoshop depends on the subject matter of the image. Blends and skin tones that should appear soft, not harsh, should not be oversharpened. Images with very defined edges usually benefit from more unsharp masking, while an image with overall flat color may adopt an undesirable pattern if you apply the Photoshop Unsharp Mask filter.

In general, *oversharpening*—that is, the application of too much unsharp masking—makes things look unrealistic and tends to intro-duce halos where the edges have been adjusted. The three controls in the Unsharp Mask filter (Filter/Sharpen/Unsharp Mask) that deter-mine how much unsharp masking is applied are Amount, Radius, and Threshold. (See the Photoshop documentation for details.)

The effects of Unsharp Mask settings in Adobe Photoshop are more pronounced on-screen than in a printed image. Have a proof made before you go to print to ensure that the settings you have chosen are cor-rect for your image.

To sharpen certain images subtly, such as for skin tones, experiment with different Threshold values in the Unsharp Mask dialog box. Values ranging from 8-15 usually work well for skin tones.

Flesh tones need only slight adjustments to enhance the contrast in the image.

Defined edges benefit from unsharp masking, which enhances details.

Natural ingredients can easily look garish if too much unsharp masking is applied.

Using the Right Tool for the Job

Part of the power of Adobe Photoshop in prepress production is in the sheer number of tools available to the user. In fact, because of this versatility, choosing the right tool for a job is sometimes confusing. What follows are some tips about when and how to use some of the best tools in Photoshop for print production tasks.

The following techniques assume that you are familiar with the basic tools in Photoshop. If you are not, review the documentation that comes with the program.

Using Paths to Minimize File Size

Paths are straightforward PostScript files defined by simple coordinates, which makes them extremely small and compact. Using a path instead of a channel to store a mask can reduce the size of your files. The key to using a path to store a simple mask is keeping the path simple. Soft-edged items, complex silhouettes, blends, and gradations can't be stored as paths. If the path is too complex, you will get a limit-check error when you try to print the file from Photoshop (see Appendix, "Utilizing PostScript").

Using Paths to Make Selections

A path is an excellent alternative to using the lasso tool to make selections. Typically, the lasso tool makes an irregular-edged selection, no matter how careful you are. Instead, use the pen tool to create smooth, anti-aliased paths with much cleaner results. Create paths when you need to make selections along diagonal lines or geometric shapes.

Selection using the lasso tool

Selection using the path tool

Using Paths with Painting Tools

A path can be stroked with any of the painting tools. Paths give the tool a track to follow and eliminate any wobbly strokes you might make by hand when using a more cumbersome tool such as a fat brush. Paths are particularly useful when using the dodge/burn tool. Using paths, you won't linger in any one spot; therefore, you can't overdodge or overburn an area. You can also repeat precise strokes over the same path to build up effects gradually.

Path for dodging

Dodging applied to path

Using Selection Masks

A selection mask lets you change a selected region without altering the rest of the image. Selection masks are the key building blocks for all complex compositing in Adobe Photoshop. You can use these masks to make solid or semitransparent masks; semitransparent masks work best when you need to blend an object gradually into another area.

Original foreground

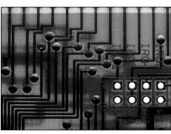

Original background

Semitransparent mask

Originals and mask combined

Using a Selection to Make a Drop Shadow

To make a drop shadow from a selected item, copy the selection, then position the copy, fill it with a color, and blur it to soften the edges. The shadow can be black or any color you want; check with your printer before making multicolored drop shadows, though, since they can create registration problems during printing.

1. Open the background image on which you want to place your object and a drop shadow. Open the Layers palette (Window/ Palettes/Show Layers); this image appears as the Background layer.

2. Open the file containing the object that needs a drop shadow. Make the object a selection, then copy the selection.

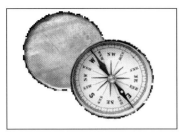

3. Highlight the window of the background image. Choose Edit/Paste Layer. In the Make Layer dialog box, name this layer (we called it Compass Layer). Click OK. The object appears as a new layer in the Layers palette of the background image.

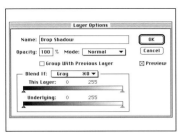

4. Copy the object layer by dragging it to the new layer icon. Double-click on the copy layer and rename it Drop Shadow in the Layer Options dialog box. Click OK.

5. Check the Preserve Transparency box in the Layers palette. Choose black (or some other color) as the foreground color and fill (Option-Delete) the Drop Shadow layer.

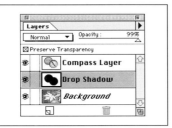

6. In the Layers palette, drag the Drop Shadow layer down between the object layer (here, Compass Layer) and the Background layer.

7. Using the move tool, position the drop shadow where you want it (in this example, we moved it down and slightly to the right).

8. Uncheck the Preserve Transparency box. Soften the edges of the drop shadow using the Gaussian Blur filter, then adjust the Opacity slider in the Layers palette. When you're satisfied with the results, save the file.

To toggle between a normal Curves grid and a finer grid, hold down the Option key and click anywhere on the grid.

Special Printing Plates

You can define specific areas for applying special printing techniques such as spot varnishes or spot colors. By saving a selection as a new channel, you can then print the channel as a separate piece of film. For example, you can use the Highlights selection in Color Range to make a special plate for printing a spot gloss varnish. As another example, you can select Reds in Color Range and use the selection as a touchplate to get very brilliant reds during printing.

Using Color Range to Make a Mask

Certain images lend themselves to using separate colors or combinations of colors to make masks. In this example, the sunglasses are made up mostly of blue. By isolating the blue, you can easily make a mask for the sunglasses. You can also add other colors to build more complex masks using Color Range.

1. Open the image containing the object you want to make a mask of. Using the lasso tool, make a rough selection just outside the object.

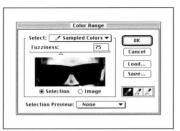

2. Choose Color Range from the Select menu; the Color Range dialog box appears. Move it to the side so you can see your image. In the dialog box, make sure the Select pop-up menu is set to Sampled Colors and that you click the Selection button.

3. Click on the predominant color in your selection with the plain eyedropper in the Color Range dialog box.

4. To add more pixels to the selection, place the eyedropper either on the image selection or on the mask in the Color Range dialog box; click while holding down the Shift key. (To delete pixels, hold down the Command key while clicking the eyedropper.)

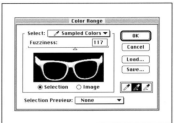

5. Once your selection mask looks nearly correct, move the Fuzziness slider in the Color Range dialog box to fine-tune the mask. When the mask looks correct, click OK.

6. If you want to reuse the selection, choose Select/Save Selection and save it as a new channel.

Using Layers for Compositing Elements

The Layers feature in Adobe Photoshop 3.0 provides a wide range of options for managing objects, images, and type. (See the Photoshop 3.0 documentation for more information about layers.)

A common production request is to composite a number of components from different images into one. For instance, if you are creating an ad for a client who is not sure of which products to include or how they should be positioned, you can anticipate some hefty prepress charges to make these changes during film production. If you composite the components yourself using layers, however, you could produce the ad more economically, show the client intermediate proofs, make changes, and control the entire compositing process.

1. Open the image you will use as the background, then open the Layers palette (Window/Palettes/Show Layers).

2. Open the file containing the first item that you want to place on the background. Make it a selection using any of the selection tools.

3. With the move tool, drag and drop the selected item onto the background file. It then becomes the Floating Selection layer in the Layers palette.

4. Choose Make Layer from the Layers palette pop-up menu; the Make Layer dialog box appears. Name the layer (Green Beans in this example). Click OK. The Floating Selection layer becomes your first layer.

5. Position the item against the background with the move tool.

6. Repeat steps 2–5 for each new element until all elements are placed against the background.

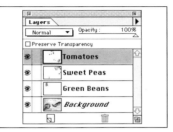

7. Save a copy of this file (choose File/Save a Copy) in Photoshop 3.0 format using the suffix *.unmerged* (in Windows, limit suffixes to three letters—*.unm*, for instance). This file contains all the layers in unmerged form so you can make changes to individual layers.

8. To make drop shadows, first deselect the eye icons of the layers that don't need them. Then follow steps 4–8 on page 43 to make each drop shadow. Choose Merge Layers in the Layers palette pop-up menu to merge the individual drop shadows.

9. Save a copy of the drop-shadow file in Photoshop 3.0 format using the suffix *.shadow*. Then choose Flatten Layers from the Layers palette pop-up menu. Save the file and make a proof for approval.

10. If you need to change individual elements, open the *.unmerged* file and add, change, or delete items as necessary. (If only the drop shadow needs adjusting, open the *.shadow* file and make your changes there.)

When compositing many selections using Layers, you can make an individual drop shadow for each selection before placing them on a background. If you have many items to place, however, this could take a long time. Instead, merge just the layers that need drop shadows and make a drop shadow for all of the elements at once.

To view the contents of the layer mask only, Option-Click on the layer mask icon; to return to viewing the image, Option-Click on the layer image.

Using Layers to Combine Images

Images with too much contrast or inappropriate detail can be edited using either two scans of the original that each capture different areas of the scene or two exposures of the same image, scanned separately. Either method allows you to capture the best detail from each. In this example, we combine the highlights from one image with the shadows of another.

1. Open the two images you want to combine (make sure they have the same resolution and are cropped exactly the same). Then open the Layers palette (Window/Palettes/Layers).

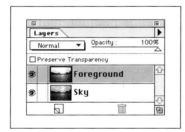

2.Using the move tool, drag and drop one image on top of the other; the image on top becomes Layer 1. Close the original file of that image.

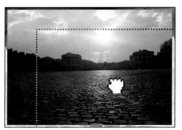

3. To name the layers, double-click on the Background layer in the Layers palette; a dialog box appears. Rename the Background layer (here, it's called Sky); click OK. Then double-click on Layer 1 and name it (Foreground in this example). Click OK.

4. To combine elements from both layers, make a layer mask. Select the top layer (Foreground), then choose Add Layer Mask from the pop-up menu. A blank thumbnail appears next to the image in the Layers palette. This is the layer mask.

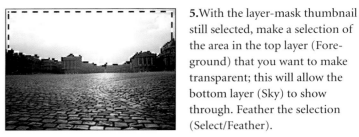

5.With the layer-mask thumbnail still selected, make a selection of the area in the top layer (Foreground) that you want to make transparent; this will allow the bottom layer (Sky) to show through. Feather the selection (Select/Feather).

6. Make sure the foreground color is black, then use it to fill the selection (Option-Delete). You can see the change in the thumbnail. This creates a temporary mask that allows the bottom layer to show through the selection. Deslect (⌘D).

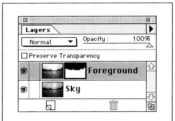

7. You can reveal more detail from the bottom layer by adding to the layer mask. In this example, we double-clicked on the paintbrush tool, set the opacity to 50%, and chose a medium-soft brush in the Brushes palette.

8. With the layer mask still selected, paint the areas on the top image to expose detail from the same areas on the bottom image. Here, we brightened the highlights in the Foreground layer using pixels from the Sky layer.

9. When you have finished editing your image, combine the layers by choosing Flatten Image from the Layers palette pop-up menu. Save the image.

46

Using HSB Values to Match Colors

From time to time, you may be confronted with the problem of using items of similar colors that were photographed under different conditions. Here, we show two neutral-colored products that need to be placed on the same spread in a brochure. The colors differ in the original transparencies but must match in the brochure.

1. Open the image that needs a color change.

2. Make a selection of the portion of the image you want to change

3. Open the second image with the color that you want the first image to match.

4. Open the Info palette and choose Palette Options from the pop-up menu; the Info Options dialog box appears. To view HSB (hue, saturation, and brightness) values, select HSB Color from the Mode pop-up menu in the Second Color Readout section.

5. Using the eyedropper tool (with the Sample Size in the Eyedropper Options palette set to 3 by 3 Average), sample the color you want to match (midtone colors are best). Note the HSB values in the Info palette for the color you select. Click OK.

6. Activate the window of the image that needs the color change and hide the selection (⌘H). Open the Hue/Saturation dialog box (⌘U). Check the Colorize box to reset the Hue to 0 and the Saturation to 100.

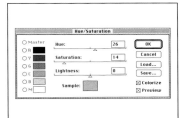

7. Enter the hue and saturation values you found in step 5. If the hue value is greater than 180, subtract 360 from that value and enter the negative result. Leave the Lightness value at 0.

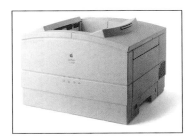

8. If the image needs further adjustment to match the colors, move the Hue and Saturation sliders slightly until the colors match as you want.

9. If you need to change other images to this color, save the settings in the Hue/Saturation dialog box to load later. Click OK. The selection is painted with the new color and the brightness value of the pixels is preserved.

When you drag and drop a floating selection to a layer or another image, hold down the Option key to drop it in the top left-hand corner, or hold down the Shift key to drop it in the center.

Using Two Windows

It is sometimes difficult to see the effects of certain image editing techniques such as airbrushing, dodging and burning, and subtle color correction. If this is the case, you can work on an extreme close-up of the image while the full view of the same image is open in a second window. This enables you to work in finely detailed areas while seeing the effects on the overall image. To do so, select Window/ New Window; a second window showing the same image will appear. Zoom in to an extreme close-up of the image to perform editing tasks.

Using Gaussian Blur to Reduce Graininess

Sometimes scanned images have more graininess than you would like. This can happen if you have scanned a grainy print or if you have greatly enlarged an image during scanning. Also, certain color channels may be grainier than others due to the way photographic films are made. You can apply the following technique to an image overall or to an individual color channel if it is grainier than the others. For instance, if your blue channel is grainy (which it often is), apply the Gaussian Blur filter to just the blue channel to reduce the graininess in it and to improve final image reproduction.

1. Open the original grainy image.

2. Choose Gaussian Blur (Filter/ Blur/Gaussian Blur) to blur the image. Select a Radius of 0.5 to start (as we did); adjust it up or down as needed. (For very grainy images, you can apply the Gaussian Blur filter twice.)

3. Choose Sharpen Edges (Filter/ Sharpen/Sharpen Edges) to the image to retrieve sharpness after blurring. Reapply the Sharpen Edges filter until you achieve the effect you want.

Converting Color Images to Grayscale

The most common way to convert color images to grayscale is simply to convert your color image to Grayscale mode. At times, however, Calculations (Image/Calculations) may give your images better tonal range and less graininess. In the bottom group of images, for example, we examined the three RGB channels in grayscale. Using Calculations, we then blended just the Red and Green channels with a 30% screen.

Original RGB image

Converted to Grayscale mode

Red channel

Green channel

Red and Green channels screened at 40%

Blue channel   *Calculations*

Fine-Tuning CMYK Images

If you haven't already done so, you must convert your RGB image to CMYK mode for printing. This process converts the three RGB channels to the four process-color channels. With your RGB image open, simply choose CMYK Color from the Mode menu. Keep in mind that all Preferences—Monitor Setup, Printing Inks Setup, and Separation Setup—must be set before you convert from RGB to CMYK (see Chapter 6, "Preparing and Printing Files").

Using Channels to Fine-Tune CMYK Images

If you perform most of your color corrections in RGB mode and then convert to CMYK, you might find that the conversion introduces subtle color shifts in the form of either a color cast or an overall darkening of the image. You can use Curves to adjust each channel individually or in combination with others and to fine-tune these images before printing (see pages 34–40 as well as the *Adobe Photoshop 3.0 Tutorial* for information on adjusting curves).

1. Open the CMYK image you want to adjust.

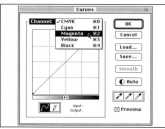

2. Choose Image/Adjust/Curves; the Curves dialog box appears. Make sure the Preview box is checked. In the Channel pop-up menu, choose the first channel that needs adjustment.

3. Adjust the curve and view the changes in the composite image.

4. If needed, select other channels to adjust. Once the image is as you want it, click OK.

Variation: If you want to work on more than one channel at once, open the Channels palette and select the first channel you want to adjust.

To add other channels you want to adjust in combination with the first, hold down the Shift key while clicking on the additional channels. Click on the eye icon next to the composite channel.

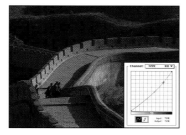

Open the Curves dialog box and make adjustments to the combined channels as needed. When the adjustments are complete, click OK.

You can edit one channel at a time while viewing changes in the composite channel. In the Channels palette, click on the individual channel you want to edit, then click on the eye icon of the composite channel.

Using Selective Color to Fine-Tune CMYK Images

Selective color correction lets you modify a specific color by changing the amounts of inks used to make it. The Selective Color command in Adobe Photoshop 3.0 allows you to make selective color corrections similar to those done on high-end prepress systems. Unlike the high-end systems, which adjust only CMYK and RGB colors, Photoshop 3.0 also lets you adjust neutrals, whites, and blacks.

Adjustments can be made to an entire image or to individual selections. In this example, the neutral background and the red petals were each adjusted using Selective Color. In general, Selective Color affects bright, saturated colors more than lighter ones. It is usually best to make selective color adjustments on CMYK images so your adjustments will closely match your printed output.

1. With the CMYK image open and the composite channel selected, choose Image/Adjust/ Selective Color; the Selective Color dialog box appears. Check the Preview box and move the dialog box so you can see your image while you work.

2. Choose a color to adjust from the Colors pop-up menu. To adjust the background in this image, we selected Neutrals. Move the sliders to make adjustments. (We adjusted the Magenta and Yellow sliders.)

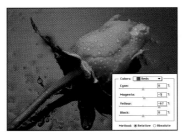

3. To adjust another color, choose it from the Colors pop-up menu and adjust the sliders. We chose Reds to increase the percentage of red in the petals of the rose. Click OK when the image is as you want it.

Matching Backgrounds in Adobe Photoshop

To precisely match or extend a background color in an Adobe Photoshop file while minimizing the file size, sample the color, create or extend the background area, then fill it with a low-resolution version of that color. Attempting to create the background in another application sometimes results in slightly different output values than those in the Photoshop file, even if you use the same percentage values shown in Photoshop. In this example, we are extending the red background color on all sides of the image.

1. Open the CMYK image that contains your background color.

2. Using the eyedropper tool while holding down the Option key, sample the color you want for your background. (By holding the Option key, this color becomes your background fill color.)

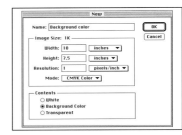

3. Create a new file and enter the dimensions needed for your background, a 1-ppi resolution, CMYK Color mode, and Background Color (in the Contents box). Click OK.

4. Save both files in EPS format and place them in your page layout program for output.

Dodging and Burning Images

In Adobe Photoshop, you can lighten or darken specific areas of an image to enhance areas of interest, much as traditional photographers do when they dodge and burn in the darkroom. To make these adjustments, use the dodge/burn tool, Curves, or Layers. The dodge/burn tool works best on small areas, while large areas that might be difficult to dodge or burn evenly benefit most from the Curves method. To avoid overdodging or overburning an area, work on a layer first, then merge the layer with your image.

Using the Dodge/Burn Tool

1. Open the file that needs dodging or burning. In this image, the man's hands and face need dodging (lightening).

2. To dodge small areas of the image, double-click on the dodge/burn tool. The Toning Tools Options palette appears. Choose Dodge from the Tool pop-up menu. Set the tonal value to Midtones and adjust the exposure setting (we chose 35%).

3. Choose a soft brush from the Brushes palette and dodge the area you want to lighten using smooth, even strokes.

Using Curves

1. To dodge or burn a large area evenly, make a selection of the area you want to adjust (here, we chose the background). Choose Hide Edges (⌘H) to hide the selection border so you can see your image more easily while making adjustments.

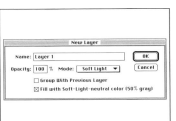

2. To dodge or burn the selection, choose Curves (Image/Adjust Curves); the Curves dialog box appears. Check the Preview box, then dodge or burn your selection by adjusting the curve in the appropriate tonal region (we darkened the midtone region).

Using Layers

1. Open the Layers palette. Choose New Layer from the Layers palette pop-up menu. Select Soft Light from the Mode menu and check the Fill with Soft-Light-neutral color (50% gray) box. Click OK.

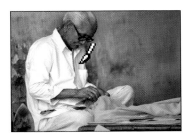

2. Set the Foreground color to black for burning, or white for dodging. Double-click the paintbrush tool and set your opacity. Select the Brushes palette and choose a soft brush. Paint the area you want to dodge or burn (we darkened the shirt and pants).

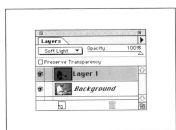

3. The dodge or burn adjustments affect the layer only, without altering your original file. If you want to make changes you can edit the layer.

4. When your image looks as you want, choose Merge Layers from the Layers palette pop-up menu.

Apply the dodge/burn tool in a sweeping motion while holding down the mouse button. If you click more than once while using the tool, not only might the effects look choppy, you also won't be able to use Edit/Undo to correct them.

Using Type

Digital Type Basics

Setting Good-Looking Type

Using Multiple Master Typefaces

Using Type

Until the advent of desktop publishing, few of us ever thought about the intricacies of typesetting. Now this task, once performed by highly trained individuals, is literally in our hands.

Although you may already have a basic understanding of how to use type on a computer, this chapter provides technical information about the characteristics of digital type, along with certain system-management tips, that should help your work go more smoothly.

This chapter also presents fundamental concepts for producing typographically sound pages, with particular emphasis on the use of multiple master typefaces and how they can enhance the way you use type.

Digital Type Basics

In the world of electronic production, type should display well on-screen and print flawlessly from output devices such as laser printers and imagesetters. Unlike type that is cast in metal or imaged photographically, PostScript Type 1 fonts and other digital type give you the means to control every aspect of typesetting.

When you buy an Adobe typeface for either the Macintosh or Windows platform, Adobe Type Manager (ATM) is also included. A basic understanding of how type renders on-screen and in print using ATM will help you produce more eloquent printed pages. This section assumes that you have installed and are using ATM.

Typesetting Terms

When older typesetting methods gave way to desktop publishing, certain traditional terms got tangled in the process. This discussion is intended to clarify the meanings of some common type terms that have been misused or have broader meanings than they did in the days of metal or photoset type.

Typefaces. The basic building block in typesetting is a *character*—a letter, number, or symbol; groups of characters are called *character sets.* One or more character sets sharing particular design features make up a *typeface design;* Adobe Caslon, for example, is the name of a typeface design.

A complete character set reflecting one stylistic variation of a typeface design, such as italic or bold, is known as a *typestyle* (see also "Fonts"

below). Basic typestyles may be combined to form new ones, such as the Adobe Caslon Bold Italic typestyle shown here. (This is the standard character set for the Macintosh; the character set you can access depends on your application and your hardware platform.)

ABCDEFGHIJKLMNOPQRSTUVWXYZ
abcdefghijklmnopqrstuvwxyz&0123456789
ÆÅÁÂÄÀÃÇÉÊËÈÍÎÏÑŒÓÔÖÒÕØÚ
ÛÜÙæáâäàåãçéêëèfiflíîïìñœóôöòøßúûüù
ÿ£¥$¢¤™©®@ao†‡§¶*!¡?¿.,.;;'''""…'"‹›«»()[]
{}|/\-‒—_•´`¨˜°˚˜¸ˆ˝˛#%‰=-+~<±>÷¬°^/·

Adobe Caslon Bold Italic typestyle

When several typestyles share a particular typeface design, they make up a typeface family. The Adobe Caslon typeface family, for instance, is made up of regular, italic, bold, and other typestyles of the Adobe Caslon typeface design.

A multiple master typeface is essentially one typeface family from which hundreds of stylistic variations, called multiple master instances, can be generated (see "Using Multiple Master Typefaces," page 61).

Fonts. In traditional metal type, *font* described a single point size of a particular typestyle and typeface design. Since digital-typesetting technology enables scalable fonts, however, today the size distinction is not always applicable. For example, Adobe Caslon Italic as a whole is considered both a scalable font and a typestyle; each instance of a multiple master typeface is also a scalable font and a typestyle. However, each point size of the bitmapped (for screen display) version of Adobe Caslon Italic is considered a distinct though nonscalable font (but not a typestyle).

Outline fonts (also known as *printer fonts*) are the means by which digital type is scalable. (On the Windows platform, outline fonts are called *.pfb* files [primary font binary].) They are created using code that describes the ideal outline of each character in mathematical terms. By adjusting the mathematical formulas, your computer can scale the point size of a character without distortion. Outline fonts generate smooth output both on-screen (in conjunction with ATM) and from your PostScript printer. If it is not resident in your printer, install the outline fonts you intend to print on your computer.

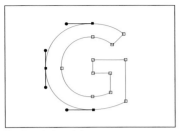 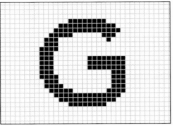

Outline (printer) font | *Bitmapped (screen) font*

As with all digital images, fonts are displayed on-screen as bitmapped representations; thus, *bitmapped fonts* are sometimes referred to as *screen fonts*. Each letter is built using a pattern of dots (pixels) that together represent the letter at a specific point size. On the Macintosh, bitmapped fonts are often kept in font "suitcases." On a Windows platform, bitmapped fonts are created dynamically by ATM.

Adobe Type Manager

The Adobe Type Manager font utility automatically generates any size bitmapped font from outline-font data. By rasterizing the outlines, ATM translates them into digital bitmaps so they can be represented on-screen. With ATM, you can scale, rotate, and skew type without the characters appearing jagged (the degree of smoothness is determined by the monitor resolution). ATM also lets you print Type 1 fonts on non-PostScript printers, such as the Hewlett-Packard DeskWriter or the Apple StyleWriter.® (See also Chapter 1, "Working Efficiently.")

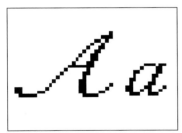 

72-dpi screen display without ATM | *72-dpi screen display with ATM*

Printer Memory

A PostScript printer's random access memory (RAM) is used to store downloaded fonts, to scale fonts, and to render an entire page of a document. This discussion focuses on font storage.

Virtual memory. Only a portion of a printer's total RAM, known as *virtual memory,* is available for storage of downloadable fonts. The amount of virtual memory varies from printer to printer, but in most

cases you can increase it by adding more RAM. Contact your printer manufacturer first, though, because there may be a maximum amount of virtual memory that can be created, regardless of total RAM. You can also store fonts on a hard drive attached to your printer, which will free up the printer's virtual memory.

In general, multiple master fonts use two to three times more virtual memory than their corresponding non–multiple master fonts. For example, the ITC Avant Garde Book typestyle requires 28KB of virtual memory, while the ITC Avant Garde Gothic multiple master font needs 68KB (each additional instance only requires about 3KB more virtual memory). The more fonts used on a page, the greater the chance you'll have problems printing that page.

Determining the amount of virtual memory. At times you may need to find out how much virtual memory your printer has. Although it's difficult to determine the amount of virtual memory in a Windows system, most printers produce a startup or self-test page that indicates total RAM. If you use a Macintosh computer, however, use the PSPrinter or LaserWriter driver (version 8.0 or greater), as follows:

1. Open Chooser and select PSPrinter (or LaserWriter 8.0 or greater). Select the output device you want to work with. Click on the Setup button.

2. Click on More Choices if the Printer Info button does not appear. Click on Printer Info.

3. Click on Update Info. The driver will query the device and display the results in the scroll box.

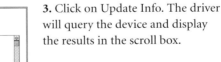

4. Scroll to Total Memory Installed, which tells you how much total RAM is in the printer. Total Memory Available tells you how much of that RAM is available for downloadable fonts.

Searching for Fonts

When you send a document to a PostScript printer, it searches for fonts in the following order:

1. Fonts that have been manually downloaded to the printer's RAM.

2. Fonts stored in the read-only memory (ROM) of the printer.

3. Fonts stored on a hard disk in or attached to the printer.

4. Fonts stored in the Macintosh or Windows system (these are downloaded by the printer driver when the job is sent to the printer).

5. The printer will use Courier if it can't find the font used in the document.

Key Font Components

Fonts are made up of several types of files; the file categories differ for Macintosh and Windows versions. Here are brief descriptions of two key font components:

Printer Font Metrics (PFM) file: A Windows-specific file developed by Microsoft. It contains character dimensions and related information that applications need to position characters on a page. Although included in some Windows font packages, PFM files are generally created by ATM during font installation.

Adobe Font Metrics (AFM) file: In Windows, ATM uses AFM and other files to make PFM files when installing a font. AFM files are also supplied with Macintosh fonts, but few users install them since no Macintosh application uses them. In UNIX systems, AFM files are used by Display PostScript to position characters on a page.

Setting Good-Looking Type

A sculpture's success depends not only on its shape and material, but also on the space around it. Typography is no different—to communicate ideas, type must be readable as well as legible. *Legibility* refers to the ability to distinguish between letters; *readability* to ease of comprehension and reader comfort. Making type more readable involves the manipulation of space around letters, words, and lines of text. (In all captions in this chapter, any fraction indicates point size [in the numerator] and leading.)

Spacing Letters

As we read a line of text, our eyes scan the upper third of the letters. From this information, we identify the overall word shapes, which we quickly comprehend as thoughts and meaning within context. When the spaces between pairs of letters (*letterfit*) are optically even overall, it allows us to recognize the forms of letters (*letterforms*) without distraction, which in turn enables us to identify words easily.

The characteristics that make a letter legible are shape, proportion, stroke contrast, and letterfit. Although the unique shape of an individual letter helps make it legible, it may also create undesirable letterfit. Thus, the spatial relationship between two or more characters is a major factor in determining a word's readability.

Letterfit. To help you determine the proper spacing between any two letters, envision the space within a letterform (its *counterform*) and the space between it and its neighbor (its *letterfit*) as physical volumes. The default letterfit of most text typefaces tries to visually balance these volumes so that an even rhythm of white space is achieved.

The shapes of individual letters influence letterfit. For instance, two letters with either curved or diagonal strokes that are set together require the least amount of space between them; combinations of straight vertical lines need the most space; and a curved or diagonal stroke next to a straight line needs a medium amount of space.

The amount of space between letters depends on the shapes of the letter strokes.

Tracking. Adding or removing an equal amount of space between characters, usually in blocks of text, to achieve overall tighter or looser *letterspacing* is known as *tracking*. Type smaller than 10 points might require added space (*positive tracking*), while larger type sizes—say, over 18 points—might need less (*negative tracking*). Most page layout programs include tracking capabilities; the way you perform this function varies by application, so refer to your user guide for details.

A Crow, half-dead with thirst, came upon a Pitcher which had once been full of water, but when the Crow put its beak into the mouth of the Pitcher

Tracking: −25 (Octavian MT, 18 points)

A Crow, half-dead with thirst, came upon a Pitcher which had once been full of water, but when the Crow put its beak into the mouth of the Pitcher he found that only very little water was left and that he could not reach far enough down to get at it. He tried, and tried, but at last had to give up in despair. Then a thought came to him, and he

Tracking: +12 (Octavian MT, 10 points)

Reversed type, such as white type on a black background, might also require more space between letters. In this case, use positive tracking (or less negative tracking, as shown here) to improve legibility.

Tracking: −40 (Inflex Bold, 28/36)   *Tracking: −20 (Inflex Bold, 28/36)*

Your printing environment may also require adjustment of the overall letterspacing. If you are printing on an absorbent paper, for instance, you may need to increase letterspacing to allow for ink spread that occurs during printing. If so, use positive tracking.

Kerning. Altering the space between any two characters is known as kerning. Many problematic character combinations are adjusted by the typeface designer or manufacturer; these kerning pairs are included with the typeface software. Most Adobe typefaces, for instance, have 294 standard kerning pairs; Adobe Originals™ designs have many more—sometimes thousands.

Ta rv We gy RA 7, y.

Unkerned character pairs (Centaur MT, 20 points)

Ta rv We gy RA 7, y.

Kerned character pairs (Centaur MT, 20 points)

Many applications let you kern letter pairs manually; some are also capable of using the built-in kerning pairs automatically. If your application allows it and does not do so already, make sure the built-in kerning pairs are accessible as the default in the application. Check your user guide for details.

Manual kerning. At times you may need to kern manually to balance the letterfit with the counterforms for visual consistency. You may need to kern, for example, if you use all capitals or if you work with unusual letter combinations.

Capital letters are generally designed to fit well with lowercase letters, and so may look tight or uneven when set together. Nevertheless, there are times when all capitals best convey your message, though they will undoubtedly require adjustment. As always, try to balance the letters' counterforms with the space around them, first by globally tracking the words or lines of text, then by kerning the spaces between certain pairs of characters.

The following pair of examples shows manually kerned spacing between capital letters. In the first example, the capital letters are set using default spacing; in the second (after kerning and tracking), the spaces between the letter pairs are more evenly balanced with the counterforms.

CLIMATE

Before manual kerning: uneven letterfit (Adobe Caslon Regular)

CLIMATE

After manual kerning and tracking: more balanced spacing (Adobe Caslon Regular)

Unusual letter combinations, which crop up in work with languages other than English or in situations in which there are no predefined kerning pairs, can cause letters to tangle, distracting the eye. Add space where letters "crash," as shown in this example (*igjen* is the Norwegian word for *again*).

igjen   **igjen**

Before kerning (Adobe Caslon Semibold)   *After kerning (Adobe Caslon Semibold)*

Spacing Words

Words need to be far enough apart to be distinguished from one another, but not so far that they separate into individual, unrelated units. The spaces between words have to be large enough to see individual word shapes, but the reader must also be able to group three or four words at a time for quick comprehension. The proper word spacing for *unjustified* text (in which the right margin is uneven or *ragged*) depends primarily on type size and line length.

If headlines are set in a large-size type—24 points, for example—little space is required between words; the space used by a 24-point lowercase *i* is a good gauge. In typical 12-point body text of ten words per line, however, more space between words is required. Most page layout programs use the default word spacing provided in each typeface, which usually works well without adjustment in typical text settings, and some allow you to adjust this spacing. Very short lines of text require tighter word spacing than the default.

A Jay ventured into a yard

Headline word spacing (Myriad multiple master 700 weight 500 width, 24 points)

If one spacing parameter changes on the page, then the others should change accordingly. If you increase the spaces between the words and letters, for instance, you need to increase the leading as well.

To find out what the kerning pairs are in a particular typeface, open the typeface's AFM file in a text editing program. Kerning pairs are enumerated after the line reading *StartKernData*. The number of kerning pairs will be given at the line reading *StartKernPairs [X]*, where *[X]* represents the number of kerning pairs.

Font Size

Fonts set at the same point size may vary in actual size; for example, not all 12-point fonts appear to be the same size. The transition from metal and photo-set type to digital type has left us with a few idiosyncrasies, and this is one of the more vexing. The apparent size of a typeface depends largely on the height of the lowercase letters and the sizes of their counterforms.

abcd
Futura Condensed

abcd
Catull Regular

abcd
ITC Avant Garde Gothic multiple master

abcd
Bernhard Modern Roman

abcd
Diotima Roman

abcd
Snell Roundhand

Spacing Lines

The spacing between lines, known as *leading* from metal type, is determined in part by line length and type size. The proper amount of leading gracefully guides the eye from the end of one line to the beginning of the next; too much or too little leading fails at this purpose.

A Jay ventured into a yard where Peacocks used to walk and found there a number of feathers which had fallen from the Peacocks when they were moulting. He tied them to his tail and strutted down towards the Peacocks. As the Jay approached, the Peacocks discovered the disguise and pecked at the Jay and plucked away his borrowed plumes. So when the Jay went back to the other Jays, who had watched his behavior from a distance, they were equally annoyed with him and told him: "It is

Too little leading (ITC Flora, 8/8.5)

A Jay ventured into a yard

where Peacocks used to walk

and found there a number

of feathers which had fallen

from the Peacocks when they

Too much leading (ITC Flora, 8/34)

Line length. When setting body text, keep in mind that too long a line tends to tire the eye and makes it difficult to locate the beginning of the next line; on the other hand, lines that are too short can disrupt sentence structure. Generally, a line of body text has fifty-five to sixty-five characters (nine to ten words) for optimum legibility. Captions are often set in shorter lines.

Determining leading. If your line length is typical for body text—that is, about ten words long in 12-point type—first try using leading that is 2 points larger than the type size. If your type is larger than 12 points or has longer lines, the spacing between the lines should also be larger. Another method is to set the leading at 120% of the type size—increase this percentage slightly if the words-per-line count is higher than the norm and decrease the percentage if it is lower. Leading is also influenced by the tracking and word spacing in your document. As a rule of thumb, the white space between lines should be larger than the word spacing to encourage the reader's eye to travel along one line before going to the next.

Setting justified text. Lines that have even left and right margins are called *justified*. The word spacing in justified text usually needs to be handled carefully to look good. Using hyphenation and justification (H&J) algorithms, most page layout programs automatically break words using hyphens and adjust the letterspacing and word spacing to

justify the lines; excessive use of word breaks and spacing adjustments, however, can produce a text block that is difficult to read, as in the example on the right. Generally, little or no letterspacing adjustment should be used in justified text. If you need to, though, you can usually fine-tune the application's default H&J values manually. Try to avoid "rivers" of white space running through your justified text.

A Jay ventured into a yard where Peacocks used to walk and found there a number of feathers which had fallen from the Peacocks when they were moulting. He tied them to his tail and strutted down to-wards the Peacocks. As the Jay ap-proached, the Peacocks discovered the disguise and pecked at the Jay and plucked away his borrowed plumes. So when the Jay went back to the other Jays, who had watched his behavior from a distance, they

Good justification (ITC Flora, 8/12)

A Jay ventured into a yard where Peacocks used to walk and found there a number of feathers which had fallen from the Peacocks when they were moulting. He tied them to his tail and strutted down towards the Peacocks. As the Jay approached, the Peacocks discovered the disguise and pecked at the Jay and plucked away his borrowed plumes. So when the Jay went back to the other Jays, who had

Poor justification (ITC Flora, 8/12)

Professional Polish

There are a few subtle typesetting techniques that greatly enhance legibility and require little more than adjusting habits you might have learned on the typewriter.

Quotation marks. Don't use single (') or double (") prime marks for single (') and double (") quotation marks, respectively; instead, use curved "true" quotation marks. In many applications, you can access these marks automatically by using these keystrokes:

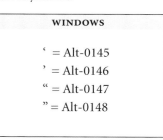

MAC	WINDOWS
' = Option-]	' = Alt-0145
' = Shift-Option-]	' = Alt-0146
" = Option-[	" = Alt-0147
" = Shift-Option-[	" = Alt-0148

Emphasis. Although the underline command is available in all desktop publishing programs, it should never be used for emphasis in text; instead, use the typeface family's italic or bold font (that is, do not create artificial italic or bold versions by selecting these options from the Macintosh or Windows typestyle menu).

Ligatures. Common ligatures were designed to rid us of such unhappy character pairs as fi and fl. Actually two or more characters combined into one, *ligatures* blend letter pairs smoothly: fi and fl. For the Macintosh, the keyboard commands for fi and fl ligatures are Shift-Option-5 and Shift-Option-6, respectively. Windows does not support ligatures in regular font sets; instead, use the corresponding Expert Set. Expert Sets also include ff, ffi, and ffl ligatures (see page 60).

five affluent floozies

Without ligatures (Bembo Regular, 28 points)

five affluent floozies

With ligatures (Bembo Regular and Bembo Expert, 28 points)

Spacing. Unlike typewriter text, which is *monospaced* (each letter occupies the same width), most digital fonts are designed with *proportional spacing*, in which the width of each character varies. Proportional spacing helps distinguish characters and makes the type easier to read. And since proportional spacing affects punctuation as well, you need only one space after the ending punctuation instead of the two required in typewriting.

```
Hal Clayton dropped off
pretty soon, but I
didn't; I wasn't ever so
wide awake in my life.
I was spying out from
under the shade of my
hat brim, searching the
floor for leather.  It
took me a long time, and
I begun to think maybe
my guess was wrong, but
at last I struck it.  It
laid over by the bulk-
```

Monospaced font (Letter Gothic, 8/11.5)

Hal Clayton dropped off pretty soon, but I didn't; I wasn't ever so wide awake in my life. I was spying out from under the shade of my hat brim, searching the floor for leather. It took me a long time, and I begun to think maybe my guess was wrong, but at last I struck it. It laid over by the bulkhead, and was nearly the color of the carpet. It was a little round plug about as thick as the end of

Proportional font (Avenir, 8/11.5)

Dashes. Use em and en dashes correctly. The width of an em dash (—) generally equals the type's point size; for example, a 6-point em dash is 6 points wide. These are used to indicate sudden breaks in thought or to signal digression, amplification, or explanation (on a Macintosh, press Shift-Option-hyphen; with Windows, press Alt-0151). En dashes (–) are half the width of em dashes and are used in ranges of numbers, such as dates or page sequences (on a Macintosh, press Option-hyphen; with Windows, press Alt-0150). Many typographers consider em dashes in body text to be visually distracting and instead use en dashes with a space on either side. Type designers have recognized this problem and now include the ¾-em dash (–) in Expert Sets.

and dog me to a good place and make me give up the di'monds, and then he'll—oh, I know what he'll do! Ain't it awful—awful! And now to think the OTHER one's aboard, too! Oh, ain't it hard luck, boys—ain't it hard! But you'll help save me, WON'T you?—oh, boys, be good to a poor devil that's being hunted to death, and save me—I'll

¾-em dashes (Centaur, 10/12.5)

and dog me to a good place and make me give up the di'monds, and then he'll—oh, I know what he'll do! Ain't it awful—awful! And now to think the OTHER one's aboard, too! Oh, ain't it hard luck, boys—ain't it hard! But you'll help save me, WON'T you?—oh, boys, be good to a poor devil that's being hunted to death, and save me—I'll

Em dashes (Centaur, 10/12.5)

Hyphenation. When hyphenated word breaks occur at the ends of three or more lines in a row, the effect is often distracting; use tracking, alternate line breaks, and other methods to remove excess hypenation. Always double-check hyphenation in a dictionary, since desktop publishing applications don't always break words correctly. Some words break awkwardly; even though they are correct, these word breaks should be avoided.

lilies standing like trum- pets in a military row

an explosion of octo- pus ink shrouded the

Correct but awkward word breaks (Futura Bold, 10/14 points)

Ellipses. Use the keyboard command for ellipses (…) rather than running three periods together. The command for the Macintosh is Option-; (semicolon); for Windows, it is Alt-0133.

Some programs offer automatic ligatures—usually for fi and fl only. The Smart Punctuation filter in version 5.5 of Adobe Illustrator (select Filter/Text/Smart Punctuation) allows you to search for and change ligatures in a document.

Title, running head, and footnotes: Adobe Caslon Regular Small Caps

Body text: Adobe Caslon Regular and Adobe Caslon Expert Regular (old style figures)

Superscripts: Adobe Caslon Expert Regular (superior figures)

Folio: Adobe Caslon Expert Semibold (old style figures)

Other design elements: Adobe Caslon Ornaments

INTRODUCTION TO A TYPEFACE

William Caslon's Types

Designed and cut by William Caslon in the 1720s and 1730s, the original Caslon types were based on the best Dutch typefaces, but improved so profoundly on the quality and form of the types that it has been said that he single-handedly changed the course of printing history.

Caslon completed work on his first fonts about 1720, but it was not until 1734 that his first specimen sheets appeared.[1]

William Caslon began his working life as an engraver of pistol and musket locks. His gift for precision work led him to the making of bookbinding stamps, tools for silver working, and eventually to the art of letter-founding, which was to make him famous in his own lifetime.

Caslon died in 1766 having designed some of the best-loved roman and italic text faces in typographic history.[2]

1. CASLON CREATED HIS TYPEFACE OVER A PERIOD OF ABOUT 20 YEARS. EVERY LETTER OF EACH SIZE AND STYLE WAS DESIGNED AND CUT BY HAND.

2. AFTER HIS DEATH, CASLON'S FOUNDRY REMAINED IN THE FAMILY FOR ANOTHER CENTURY. THE LAST CASLON, HENRY WILLIAM, DIED IN 1874.

97

Expert Collections

Before digital type, many serif text typefaces came with *old style figures*—numerals designed to harmonize with lowercase letters by having ascenders and descenders. By contrast, the regular or *lining figures* found in the standard character set are as tall as capitals and designed to be set in lines of all capitals or in tables. Sans serif typefaces also use lining figures in body text. Depending on the typeface, old style figures may be included in its Expert Collection.

The Expert Collections for Adobe Originals text typeface families include Small Caps & Old Style Figures (SC&OSF) character sets along with Expert Sets of fractions, superior and inferior figures, and an expanded set of ligatures. The SC&OSF (for the Macintosh) and Expert Set and Subset (for Macintosh and Windows) character sets of one text typeface—Bembo—are shown in the following three boxes.

SMALL CAPITALS

REGULAR

ABCDEFGHIJKLMNOPQRSTUVWXYZ
ABCDEFGHIJKLMNOPQRST
UVWXYZ1234567890
ÅÇƒ©˙˚¬øŒ®SS†¥ÅıÇÎ´Ï˝Óˆ
ÔÒÂ˜ØŒ‰Íˇ¨„¸Á˛-=[]\;',./~
!@#$%^&*()_+{}|:"<>?¡™£¢
§¶•ªº–“‘«…Æ÷⁄¤‹›FIFL‡°·‚—±”
’»ÚÆ¯˘¿ÈÉËÊÙÚÜÛÌÍÏÎÒÓÖÔÕÀÁÄ
ÂÃ`´¨ˆ˜ŸÑ

OLD STYLE FIGURES

ITALIC,
SEMIBOLD,
SEMIBOLD ITALIC,
BOLD,
BOLD ITALIC,
EXTRA BOLD, AND
EXTRA BOLDITALIC

abcdefghijklmnopqrstuvwxyz
ABCDEFGHIJKLMNOPQRST
UVWXYZ1234567890
åçƒ©˙˚¬øœ®ß†¥ÅıÇÎ´Ï˝Óˆ
ÔÒÂ˜ØŒ‰Íˇ¨„¿Á¸-=[]\;',./~
!@#$%^&()_+{}|:"<>?¡™£¢*
§¶•ªº–“‘«…æ÷⁄¤‹›fifl‡°·‚—±”’
»ÚÆ¯˘¿èéëêùúüûìíïîòóöôõàáä
âã`´¨ˆ˜ÿñ

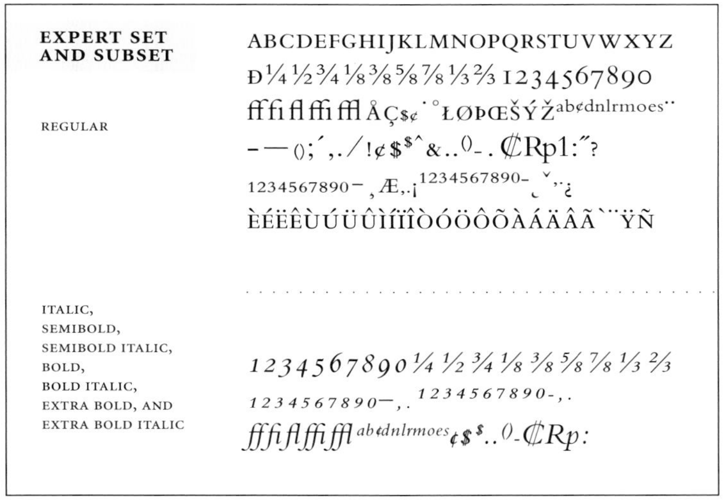

EXPERT SET AND SUBSET	ABCDEFGHIJKLMNOPQRSTUVWXYZ

Đ¼½¾⅛⅜⅝⅞⅓⅔ 1234567890

REGULAR

ff fi fl ffi ffl ÅÇsₑˊˊ˚ ŁØÞŒŠÝŽ abₑdnlrmoesˈˈ
-—0;ˊ,./!¢$ˢˆ&..0-. ₡Rp1:˝?
1234567890-ˎˎ,Æ,.¡ ¹²³⁴⁵⁶⁷⁸⁹⁰⁻ ˇˎ˚.¸¿
ÈÉÊÈÙÚÜÛÌÍÏÎÒÓÖÔÕÀÁÄÅÂ``ŸÑ

ITALIC, SEMIBOLD, SEMIBOLD ITALIC, BOLD, BOLD ITALIC, EXTRA BOLD, AND EXTRA BOLD ITALIC

1234567890¼ ½ ¾ ⅛ ⅜ ⅝ ⅞ ⅓ ⅔
1234567890—ˎˎ 1234567890-ˎˎ.
ff fi fl ffi ffl abₑdnlrmoes ₑ$ˢ..0-₡Rp:

Using Multiple Master Typefaces

Although it's always best to avoid a cacophony of typeface families on the same page, you may at times feel limited by the selection of type-styles available for any one typeface. Multiple master technology allows you to generate precisely the typeface variation, or *instance*, that you need, such as the ones shown here.

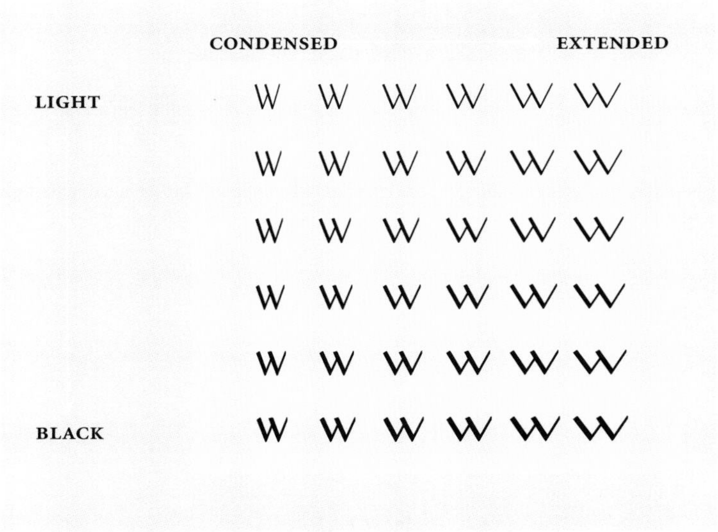

	CONDENSED					EXTENDED
LIGHT	W	W	W	W	W	W
	W	W	W	W	W	W
	W	W	W	W	W	W
	W	W	W	W	W	W
	W	W	W	W	W	W
BLACK	W	W	W	W	W	W

Some of the possible instances of Graphite multiple master

Since multiple master typefaces provide far more functionality and flexibility than ordinary typefaces, they require a little more effort to understand and use.

Primary Fonts

The set of *primary fonts* supplied with an Adobe multiple master type-face represents (and performs as) a complete typeface family. These prebuilt fonts are accessible through your application font menu after you install the typeface. The selection of primary fonts contained in each multiple master typeface is determined by the typeface designer or manufacturer, and so will vary from one typeface to another.

	CONDENSED	NORMAL	SEMI-EXTENDED
LIGHT	abc	abc	abc
REGULAR	abc	abc	abc
SEMIBOLD	abc	abc	abc
BOLD	abc	abc	abc
BLACK	abc	abc	abc

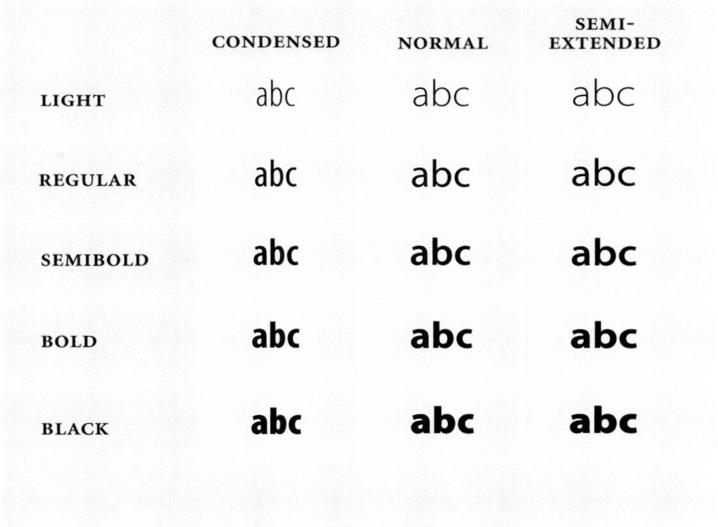

Myriad multiple master contains fifteen primary fonts

Design Axes

Two or more sets of outlines, or *master designs,* are integrated into each multiple master typeface. The master designs determine the *dynamic range,* or the difference between the extremes, of each design axis. A *design axis* is a variable typeface attribute, such as weight, width, style, or optical size. Intermediate font instances are generated by on-demand interpolation between the master designs. For example, light and bold master designs delineate the dynamic range of possible instances along the weight design axis. This means you can select a weight anywhere within this range and create a custom instance.

Prior to version 1.26, some versions of Kodak Precision ILS imagesetter-calibration software were incompatible with multiple master fonts. Users of the earlier versions will need to ask the manufacturer for an upgrade.

When you've decided to purchase a multiple master font, first make sure your printer is compatible (certain older laser printers do not work with multiple master fonts) and has enough virtual memory or a hard drive with enough capacity to accommodate the font.

Optical Size and Spacing

For most digital typefaces, overall letterspacing is optimized for 12-point text. Smaller sizes (especially 8 points or less) often require added letterspacing; larger sizes need less. The optical size design axis in a multiple master typeface will make these as well as default word-space adjustments automatically.

Each multiple master typeface incorporates from one to four design axes. Within each multiple master typeface, design axes can be used independently or in combination to generate custom instances in addition to the prebuilt primary fonts. The number of design axes and their dynamic ranges vary from one typeface to another and are determined by the type designer or manufacturer.

DESIGN AXIS	DYNAMIC RANGE
WEIGHT	a a **a a a a**
	Myriad. Light to Black
WIDTH	a a a a a a
	Viva. Condensed to Extended
STYLE	A A A A A A
	Penumbra. Sans Serif to Serif
OPTICAL SIZE	a a a a a a
	Sanvito, 6 points to 72 points (scaled to 32 points)

Optical size design axis. Metal type was made with subtle adjustments to each typeface's letter proportions, weight, stroke contrast, and spacing to optimize legibility at every point size. Digital type technologies typically do not allow this kind of variation. When a multiple master typeface has an optical size design axis, however, it is possible to generate fonts that are clear and easy to read in text sizes, yet refined and elegant in display sizes. This example shows 6-point and 72-point optically sized instances of Minion multiple master, scaled to the same size. The 6-point type has a larger *x-height* (the height of lowercase letters, excluding ascenders and descenders), heavier serifs and stems, wider characters, and looser letterfit.

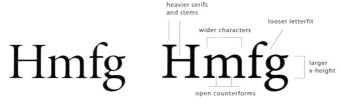

72-point Minion multiple master (scaled)   6-point Minion multiple master (scaled)

As the optical size increases, the overall spacing between characters (letterspacing) tightens, the spaces within the characters (counterforms) become smaller, the serifs become finer, the overall weight becomes lighter, and the x-height gradually decreases in size. These changes are shown below in the Sanvito multiple master typeface; when set at 10 points, the 72-optical-size letters appear too light and tightly spaced.

A Jay ventured into a yard where Peacocks used to walk and found there a number of feathers which had fallen from the Peacocks when they were moulting. He tied them to his tail and strutted down towards the Peacocks. As the Jay approached, the Peacocks discovered the disguise and pecked at the Jay and plucked away his borrowed plumes. So when the Jay went back to the

A Jay ventured into a yard where Peacocks used to walk and found there a number of feathers which had fallen from the Peacocks when they were moulting. He tied them to his tail and strutted down towards the Peacocks. As the Jay approached, the Peacocks discovered the disguise and pecked at the Jay and plucked away his borrowed plumes. So when the Jay went back to the

Sanvito 10 optical size, set at 10 points   *Sanvito 72 optical size, set at 10 points*

Weight and width design axes. Adobe's multiple master typefaces are designed to adapt to the complications that can arise in typesetting, while ensuring the integrity of the letterforms and their ultimate legibility. Although some applications allow you to artificially compress or stretch letters (often causing distortion of the letterforms), multiple master technology allows you to adjust the width of certain typefaces without distorting the letterforms. Among the common production problems that multiple master typefaces can address are headline fit and tone, reversed type, and translations.

A multiple master custom font can compensate for a headline that is too long or too short for the allotted line length—without distorting the letters (as application software might) or changing the weight or point size.

The Ant and the Grasshop

ITC Avant Garde Gothic multiple master 740 Bold 750 Normal, 20 points

The Ant and the Grasshopper

ITC Avant Garde Gothic multiple master 740 weight 600 width, 20 points

You can also create headlines whose letters are slender and light one moment and heavy and robust the next, without changing typefaces.

*feather***weight**

Caflisch Script multiple master 280 Light 640 Bold, 34 points

blackout

Viva multiple master, various weights and widths, 28 points

Reversed type should be slightly heavier than normal type to compensate for ink spread during the printing process. A simple adjustment of the weight design axis will easily solve this problem.

Ink Spread	*Ink Spread*
Caflisch Script Swash 280 Light, 29 points	*Caflisch Script Swash 400 weight, 29 points*

When text is translated in the same document, the translation usually requires a different amount of space than the original text. By adjusting the character widths slightly, however, you can often set both versions in the same amount of space. The samples below were set in Minion multiple master.

In the *Paris by Night* canvases, urban reality presents a different plastic formulation. As contrasted with *New York by Night*, most of the canvases are painted, virtually without the image/photo's assistance. As opposed to a New York swarming with threats, danger and anxiety, Latana presents a more serene city.	Dans les toiles de *Paris by Night*, la réalité urbaine présente une autre formulation plastique. A la différence de *New York by Night*, la plupart des toiles sont quasiment peintes sans le concours de l'image photo. A la différence d'un New York envahi de menaces, de dangers et d'angoisses, Latana nous met en situation une ville plus sereine.
367 weight 585 width 9 optical size, 9/13	*367 weight 500 width 9 optical size, 9/13*

Multiple Master Font Names

A multiple master font menu may appear daunting at first because of the unusual naming system used for instances. Understanding how the naming system works should help you make your font selections.

Each instance name contains one number-letter combination, such as 400 RG or 540 wt, for each design axis in the typeface. If the typeface has one design axis, for example, there is a single number-letter combination; if there are two design axes, there are two number-letter combinations; and so on.

Each number indicates the instance's position along the respective design axis; the letters indicate a primary font's style (such as regular or bold condensed) or, for custom instances, the design axis being varied (such as weight, width, or optical size). Thus, the Minion multiple master name "Myriad MM 215 LT 300 CN" indicates a light condensed primary font with a 215 weight value and a 300 width value; the name "Myriad MM 540 wt 545 wd" indicates a custom instance with a 540 weight value and a 545 width value.

	MM FAMILY	WEIGHT	WIDTH	OPTICAL SIZE
3 AXES	Minion MM	367 RG	465 CN	11 OP
2 AXES	ITC Avant Garde MM	445 RG	750 NO	
1 AXIS	Caflisch MM	280 LT		

Primary-font naming convention

	MM FAMILY	WEIGHT	WIDTH	OPTICAL SIZE
3 AXES	Minion MM	540 wt	545 wd	9 op
2 AXES	ITC Avant Garde MM	300 wt	500 wd	
1 AXIS	Caflisch MM	300 wt		

Custom-instance naming convention

If you have created an instance with a value of 12 on the optical size design axis, make sure it is also set at 12 points when you use it in your application. If you use the font at some other point size, you lose its optical correctness and its legibility could be compromised.

Penne with Puttanesca Sauce

As the story goes, the recipe for this lusty sauce was devised by certain ladies of Rome known to keep late hours. After they returned from an arduous night, this garlicky sauce was thrown together quickly with a few potent ingredients at hand. Served on hot pasta with freshly grated Parmesan, this dish was hungrily enjoyed before the cooks collapsed into bed again.

INGREDIENTS   SERVES 4 TO 6

2 lbs fresh Roma tomatoes, peeled, seeded, and coarsely chopped

2–3 anchovies, chopped fine

1/2 C oil-cured black olives; chopped

3 T capers

1 C Italian parsley, chopped

3–4 cloves garlic, peeled, smashed, and minced fine

1/2–1 tsp dried crushed chili peppers

1/2 C extra-virgin olive oil

1 lb penne

Freshly grated Parmesan cheese

PREPARATION

1   Combine all ingredients except pasta and cheese in a large bowl.

2   Let flavors meld at room temperature while pasta cooks.

3   Cook pasta al dente and drain.

4   Toss pasta with sauce; serve immediately.

5   Sprinkle liberally with Parmesan.

As you work with Adobe's multiple master typefaces, you will become familiar with the relative weights and widths the numbers represent. For example, a Myriad multiple master instance with a 222 weight value and a 697 width value indicates a light extended design; one with a 695 weight and a 315 width indicates a bold condensed instance. Both of these examples are set in Myriad.

light extended

222 weight 697 width

bold condensed

695 weight 315 width

Creating Custom Fonts

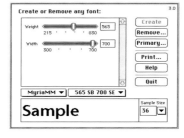

To create custom instances on a Macintosh, use the Font Creator utility supplied with each multiple master typeface. Select positions along each of the typeface's design axes in one of three ways: Drag the sliders, enter numeric values in the boxes beside the sliders, or click on the appropriate design axis to move the slider automatically to that position, then click Create. With Windows, use the Create button on the ATM Control Panel (see the *Multiple Master User Guide* for details).

Managing Custom Fonts

To conserve disk space, remove from your system any primary fonts and custom instances you are no longer using; to do so, use the Remove button in the Font Creator. The Font Creator can restore primary fonts once they are removed, but custom instances must be re-created from scratch.

If you have a font-management utility such as Suitcase and are using several custom instances that you intend to use again, you can put those instances in a separate suitcase for easy access. It's also a good idea to keep a list of custom instances used in a document.

Several graphics and page layout applications automatically re-create any instances used in your document—provided that the multiple master typefaces from which the instances are derived are installed in your system.

Using Adobe Acrobat
For Production

Introducing Adobe Acrobat 2.0

Creating PDF Files with Acrobat Distiller

Working with PDF Files

Using Adobe Acrobat

Using Adobe Acrobat For Production

Adobe Acrobat™ 2.0 is a set of tools and applications that lets you create electronic documents and share them across computer platforms. Among its production uses are reviewing, critiquing, approving, and archiving your production projects.

Since Adobe Acrobat is relatively unknown to those in the production environment, this chapter provides an overview of the products and technology, how files are converted to the Adobe Acrobat file format, and how you can apply Adobe Acrobat in everyday production.

Introducing Adobe Acrobat 2.0

Adobe Acrobat technology allows users of Macintosh, Windows, DOS, and UNIX® platforms to share electronic documents. By converting files to the Portable Document Format (PDF), for instance, a Macintosh user can share an Aldus PageMaker™ document incorporating the Utopia™ typeface with a Windows user who has neither Utopia nor PageMaker. The shared file is identical to the original, including the file's graphics, color, photographic images, fonts, and text formatting—even if the "viewing" user has none of the "creating" user's software, fonts, or type of computer.

Unlike image editing, page layout, and word processing programs, Adobe Acrobat is not a creation application. Instead, Acrobat converts application files to PDF. Users can then distribute electronic files quickly and inexpensively via conventional network and on-line systems (such as e-mail, modem, a bulletin board service [BBS], CompuServe,® or America Online®) to anyone else who also has Acrobat installed. The recipient of your Acrobat file can display and print your document with all of the color, fonts, complexity, and richness of your original file.

Adobe Acrobat 2.0 Components

Adobe Acrobat is a family of three products: Acrobat, Acrobat Pro, and Acrobat for Workgroups. Acrobat consists of the two base programs, Acrobat Reader and Acrobat Exchange. Acrobat Pro adds Acrobat Distiller™ to the base programs. Acrobat for Workgroups adds to the base programs Acrobat Distiller, an Acrobat Exchange site license for ten users, and Acrobat Catalog.

Acrobat Reader. The Acrobat Reader program is freely distributable and only allows the user to view and print PDF files. Files cannot be saved in Acrobat Reader; thus, it has none of the tools or document-enhancement features found in Acrobat Exchange.

Acrobat Exchange. The Acrobat Exchange program has a number of tools and features that enable you to view, print, annotate, search, and create hypertext links for items in a PDF document; copy text and graphics to the Clipboard; and delete, combine, or copy and rearrange pages in PDF documents. Acrobat Exchange includes the PDF Writer printer driver, which quickly converts any simple Macintosh or Windows file into a PDF file. This printer driver "prints" to an electronic file rather than a printer. It is best suited for simple business documents such as memos, letters, and spreadsheets.

Acrobat Distiller. The Acrobat Distiller program converts a PostScript file containing fonts, images, page layout, and graphics information to the Portable Document Format. It is best used for electronic documents that are complex or that contain a variety of illustrations, artwork, photographic images, or other graphic elements.

Acrobat Catalog. The Acrobat Catalog program automatically builds on-line indexes of all PDF documents on a network server, in a directory, or even on a CD-ROM. Acrobat Exchange is capable of full-text searches via the indexes produced by Acrobat Catalog.

Creating PDF Files with Acrobat Distiller

Creating PDF files from an application program is a simple two-step process: First, "print" your file as a PostScript file, then use Acrobat Distiller to convert the PostScript file to an Acrobat PDF file.

Creating a PostScript File

To create a PDF file, first "print" your original document as a PostScript file from within your creation application. The method varies by operating system and printer driver, but normally you can select File as a destination in the application's Print or Printer Setup dialog box. When asked, enter the file name with a *.ps* suffix to help differentiate the PostScript file from your original.

Converting a PostScript File to PDF

To convert your PostScript file to PDF, open the PostScript file from within Acrobat Distiller. The Save As dialog box appears. Select your file name and folder, then select Save.

This activates the Distiller program, which creates a PDF file from the PostScript file. Any user with Acrobat Exchange or Acrobat Reader can now open and view the newly created PDF file. Acrobat Distiller appends the new PDF file with a *.pdf* suffix, again to help differentiate the PDF file from the PostScript file. (The original PostScript file remains unaffected and can be redistilled or discarded.)

Before converting your PostScript file to PDF, you may want to confirm or check the compression, downsampling, and font-handling options in Acrobat Distiller. In most cases, the Distiller program's default settings are adequate. The following discussion applies if you need to change the default settings.

Compressing files. Acrobat Distiller can reduce the size of a file by as much as 90% if JPEG High is selected. Such compaction speeds network and on-line file-transfer time and expense, but can denigrate the display quality of your documents. You can, however, control the amount and type of compression through Distiller's Job Options dialog box (selected from the Distiller menu).

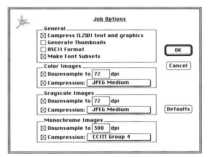

Choose either a JPEG or an LZW compression setting for color and grayscale images, CCITT for monochrome images, and LZW for text. Depending on the file's contents, the Distiller program might use multiple compression techniques.

In judging which JPEG selection to make, consider the following: JPEG Low compression specifies the least compression with minimal loss of image quality and the least reduction in file size. JPEG High compression specifies the most compression with high loss of image quality but the greatest reduction in file size.

Downsampling files. *Downsampling* (or *resampling down;* see "Resizing and Resampling Images" in Chapter 2) is another way to reduce file size; its settings are also entered in the Distiller Job Options dialog box. See the user guide for details.

Handling fonts. With Acrobat Distiller, you have the option of either embedding fonts in a file or letting the program substitute fonts for your typefaces. Embedded fonts tend to make viewing a PDF file faster because all of the font information is actually embedded in the file. Font substitution, on the other hand, relies on the Acrobat program to process and display font information.

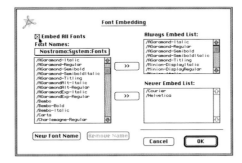

Fonts are embedded via the Acrobat Distiller Font Embedding dialog box (accessed from the Distiller menu). When you embed fonts, the PDF file's size increases by the size of the outline font file because the font information is actually incorporated into the file. Only Type 1 fonts can be embedded in PDF files via the Distiller program.

Any font selected from the Adobe Type Library may be freely embedded. For fonts outside of the Adobe Type Library, check with the original type foundry about its policy on font embedding.

Valid PostScript Files

A valid PostScript file prints pages without producing printer errors or other problems. Acrobat Distiller checks your files for any PostScript errors that the creation application may have incorporated.

To create the most efficient PostScript file, select the PostScript Level 2 option in your creation application's Print dialog box, if it is available, when creating your PostScript file.

If you get a PostScript error when distilling a file, you'll probably also get a PostScript error when sending the file to an imagesetter. Using Distiller to "soft proof" PostScript files in this manner minimizes schedule delays and helps control production budgets.

When you install Acrobat Exchange or Acrobat Reader on your computer, two fonts are installed automatically: Adobe Serif and Adobe Sans. These two multiple master fonts can emulate almost any font you might use (see "Using Multiple Master Typefaces" in Chapter 4).

When you create a PDF file, technical information about the fonts you used is included in that PDF file. When the PDF file is opened on another system, the Acrobat program reads the original fonts' technical data and substitutes multiple master instances of Adobe Sans or Adobe Serif, as appropriate.

Naming PDF Files

Many network and e-mail programs truncate long file names. When you create PDF files for multiplatform distribution via a network or e-mail system, then, the DOS file-naming convention is the safest to use. With this convention, file names are no longer than eight characters, have no spaces, and are followed by an optional period and extension of no more than three characters (for example., *filename.ext*).

When conforming a PDF file to the DOS convention, a PDF file name might change from *Q1 Profit and Loss.pdf* to *Q1PL.pdf*. Whether upper- or lowercase, the *.pdf* extension must be preserved if a PDF file is to be recognized by Windows versions of Acrobat programs.

Although the *.pdf* extension is not required for UNIX systems, files that do not have it may not display in an application's Open dialog box. Using the DOS naming convention ensures that PDF files retain the *.pdf* extension as they are transferred among computer platforms.

Creating Watched Folders

The Watched Folders feature in Acrobat Distiller provides a convenient way to collect PostScript files for distilling. Instead of opening one PostScript file at a time, assign certain folders as Watched Folders by selecting Watched Folders from the Distiller menu.

The Distiller program creates In and Out "dropbox" folders within any Watched Folder you assign. Once a PostScript file is placed in the In folder, Acrobat Distiller automatically distills it.

The distillation occurs immediately if the program is running; if not, it will take place the next time you start the Distiller application. The program then places the new PDF file (and the unchanged PostScript file) in the Out folder assigned to that Watched Folder.

Create Watched Folders for different projects and assign each Watched Folder its own Job Options parameters, such as compression and down-sampling settings, by selecting Edit Options in the Watched Folders dialog box.

When creating PostScript files in your creation application, save them directly to the In folder of the appropriate Watched Folder. Any In folder can contain dozens of files at any one time, and you can run the Distiller overnight to distill the contents of an entire In folder.

Working with PDF Files

Because Adobe Acrobat is a document-exchange program and not a file-creation program, PDF documents are generally noneditable. You cannot change or alter text or graphics from within either Acrobat Reader or Acrobat Exchange.

However, you can extract graphics from PDF files using Adobe Illustrator 5.5 for the Macintosh. And once you have created a PDF document, you can correct anything from a typographical error to major problems in a page or two without having to reprocess the entire multipage document.

Extracting Graphics from PDF Files

Adobe Illustrator 5.5 can open any single page in a PDF file to allow you to extract a graphic for reuse in other documents. If you use Acrobat for archiving (see page 71), for instance, Illustrator 5.5 becomes a dynamic mechanism for retrieving art, illustrations, and photographic images, whether for new projects or new versions of completed projects.

Enabling graphics extraction. To extract a graphic from a PDF file in Adobe Illustrator 5.5:

1. Make a copy of the original PDF file and open it in Illustrator 5.5. (PDF file names are listed in the Illustrator Open dialog box.)

2. A page-selection dialog box appears so you can choose which page of the PDF file to open (you can open only one page at a time). If you created thumbnails for the PDF file, these appear in the preview area of the dialog box, allowing you to visually scroll through the document, page by page. If you did not create thumbnails, the preview area of the box appears gray, and you will need to know the PDF file's page number to open the desired page.

3. Once you open the PDF page in Illustrator 5.5, you can copy it and paste it in other documents, or you can save it as an Illustrator or EPS file. Many images in PDF pages are tagged with an Adobe Photoshop identification when opened in Adobe Illustrator 5.5. After opening your PDF page in Illustrator, launch Photoshop from within Illustrator by holding down the Option key while double-clicking on the image. The image will open in Photoshop and can then be saved as a Photoshop file or in other formats.

Disabling graphics extraction. Acrobat Exchange 2.0 can assign security features that make Adobe Illustrator 5.5 and other PDF editing programs unable to open, extract, or alter a PDF file page. If a file with any of the following security measures is saved as a PDF file, it is not visible in the Adobe Illustrator Open dialog box. To assign security to a PDF file:

1. Open the PDF file in Acrobat Exchange 2.0. Select Save As from the File menu. Select the Security button in the Save As dialog box.

2. In the resulting dialog box, you can specify or change a file's password. You can also prevent viewers from printing the PDF file, changing the file's imposition or internal links, copying text and graphics to or pasting them from the Clipboard, or adding or changing notes.

Correcting PDF Files

If your PDF file contains errors and consists of only a single page, it's best to make your corrections in the creation application, then distill the file again with Acrobat Distiller. For multipage PDF files, two methods are available: using Adobe Illustrator 5.5 and using Acrobat Exchange's Replace Pages feature.

Using Adobe Illustrator 5.5. Use the method described in "Extracting Graphics from PDF Files," page 68, to open a copy of a PDF file page in Adobe Illustrator 5.5. Make the corrections, then resave the page in PDF by selecting Acrobat (PDF) in the Format pop-up menu.

Two issues are important to consider when using this method. First, because you are resaving the file in PDF from within Adobe Illustrator, you must have the PDF file's fonts on your system for this non-Distiller technique to work correctly. Adobe Illustrator assigns a system-level default font for fonts that are in the PDF file but not in your system. Resaving the file in PDF includes the default-font information that Illustrator assigned but that was not in the original PDF file. This substitution will change the look of the PDF file.

Second, the PDF page is decompressed when you open it in Illustrator. (This step also converts images to RGB mode; line art stays in CMYK mode.) The page remains decompressed when you resave the file in PDF, which increases, sometimes considerably, the PDF file's size.

Using Acrobat Exchange's Replace Pages feature. The Replace Pages method of correcting PDF files requires none of the precautions of the Adobe Illustrator method. By using this method, you retain optimal compression for the corrected PDF file. It also retains all hypertext links that may be included in the affected pages.

1. Open the file in the original creation application. Make the corrections to a range of consecutive pages. Create a PostScript file containing just the range of corrected pages and distill it with Acrobat Distiller using the same Job Options settings you used when the file was first converted to PDF.

2. Open the PDF file you want to correct in Acrobat Exchange 2.0.

3. From within Exchange, select Edit/Pages/Replace. Open the file with the corrected pages. In the Replace Pages dialog box, select the pages to be replaced. Click OK.

Adobe Photoshop cannot open a PDF file by itself, but you can open Photoshop-generated graphics that have been converted to a PDF file from within Adobe Illustrator (version 5.5 or later).

To create a PDF version of a simple word processing file on the Macintosh, use PDF Writer rather than Distiller. While in your word processing program, hold down the Control key as you select Print from the File menu. PDF Writer's Print dialog box appears. Save the file as a PDF file.

Using Adobe Acrobat

Two of the most immediate production uses for the electronic document capabilities of Adobe Acrobat are the client-review process and project archiving. Using electronic documents for a project's review cycles saves time and money because you don't need to print and photocopy paper versions and distribute them by mail or air carrier. Using an electronic document archive makes its contents accessible to any network user.

The Client-Review Process

Use Adobe Acrobat to exchange files containing graphics, text, and photographic images between two or more people on your review and approval distribution list. Once you have established a network connection with your client, another department, or an overseas affiliate, files can be transmitted in a matter of minutes.

A system for transferring digital files is similar to one for sending hard copies out for review. There are additional benefits with digital files, such as the ability to forward one PDF file to dozens of people on a mailing list without sending any hard copy. Setting up a digital system is relatively straightforward.

ESTABLISHING A DIGITAL CLIENT-REVIEW SYSTEM

1. Set up the network for transferring PDF files.

2. Provide the appropriate Acrobat software for viewing the PDF files to your clients and reviewers.

3. Generate a PDF file from your original document.

4. Distribute copies of the PDF file for review.

5. Reviewers make electronic comments in the PDF file and return the annotated file to you via the same network.

6. Collate corrections and append the original document.

Setting up a network. There are several network options for you and your clients, depending on your budget and your organization. Dedicated telephone and T-1 lines, ISDN lines, or Ethernet networks are ideal. If your company is large enough or if your client account is sizable, dedicated lines may already be set up for e-mail, accounting, inventory, or other nonmarketing activities. E-mail networks are

useful for sending PDF files as enclosures to a mail message. Apple Remote Access and similar applications are also efficient in transferring files to a remote-access server via a modem and normal phone lines. BBS systems such as FirstClass™ are also recommended for both Macintosh and Windows clients. Depending on the route on which the information travels, private e-mail services sometimes break up files and may not reassemble them correctly, so send a couple of test files when setting up your network.

By default, Acrobat Distiller 2.0 creates binary (8-bit) files rather than 7-bit ASCII files. In general, binary files tend to pass through networks, e-mail systems, and the Internet better than ASCII files, without being affected by on-line routers and gateways. Binary files are also smaller than their ASCII counterparts by about 20%.

If you are experiencing difficulty with network transmission of your Acrobat files, try distilling them as 7-bit ASCII files rather than using the binary-file default setting. Network protocols vary greatly depending on the on-line service and its transmission route. Some network protocols will pass files unchanged through routers and gateways only if they are in 7-bit ASCII format.

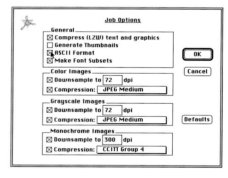

To distill PDF files as ASCII files, open the Distiller Job Options dialog box. Check the ASCII Format option under the General subheading. (When you want to retain the default settings for compression and downsampling, click Defaults first, then select the ASCII Format option.)

Providing the appropriate software. Each person in the client-review system must have either Acrobat Exchange or Acrobat Reader to view a PDF file. Acrobat Reader is a view-and-print-only application, so if your PDF proofs and drafts are meant to be annotated, saved, text-searched, cut and pasted, or anything other than viewed and printed, your entire review team needs Acrobat Exchange.

Generating a PDF file. PDF files are generated through the normal procedure described in "Creating PDF Files with Acrobat Distiller," page 66. As your project nears completion and its visual accuracy becomes more important, you might lower the compression settings in Acrobat Distiller (see "Compressing Files," page 67). Remember that higher compression means faster transmission but more denigration of image quality.

- Send initial sketches, prototypes, or drafts at high compression settings to optimize transmission performance.

- Send early proofs at medium settings as visual accuracy becomes more important.

- Send final proofs at low compression settings, or none at all, to maintain the graphic integrity of the files.

Distributing copies of the PDF file. Distribute copies of the PDF file via the network you created for this purpose. As you would with a paper draft, add a PDF cover letter to the beginning of the file to outline review procedures or to make general comments.

To create a cover letter for a review draft, use a word processing program to write your memo, then use PDF Writer rather than Distiller to create a PDF file of it. Open your main PDF file from within Acrobat Exchange, choose Edit/Pages/Insert, and open the file for your cover letter; in the Insert dialog box, place the cover letter at the beginning of the file.

Making comments. Reviewers should correct or comment on the PDF file by "attaching" electronic notes to it in Acrobat Exchange. Notes can be placed anywhere on the electronic page, and there is virtually no limit to their number. To create a note, choose Tools/Note and click on the spot where you want to place it. Type your comment in the note window, then close it. A small note icon appears on the page.

Once the note is opened (by double-clicking the note icon), the viewer sees scrollable text. Notes in Acrobat 2.0 can be customized to have different header information, colors, typefaces, and font sizes (see the user guide for details).

Request that your reviewers type in personalized headers for their notes. Or assign each reviewer a different note color—blue for editorial, green for marketing, black for legal, and so on—by selecting Edit/Preferences/Notes.

Collating corrections. Most projects have more than one reviewer. Collating their corrections is always a headache, whether you're dealing with ten marked-up paper copies or ten PDF files with notes attached. A digital solution to this paper and file shuffling is the Import option in Acrobat Exchange (select Edit/Notes/Import).

The Import Notes feature allows you to import the notes from one PDF file to a PDF file already open in Acrobat Exchange. It places those notes at the exact physical location on the same page as the one on which they were created. For example, if a note was created and placed in the middle of page 5 and you import the notes from that PDF file to a master PDF file, that note appears in the middle of page 5 of the master file. Repeat this process for each review copy with notes attached, and your master PDF file will contain all of the notes of all of the reviewers on your list.

Next, select Tools/Summarize Notes in Acrobat Exchange to summarize all notes and comments in a new, separate PDF file. The summary file lists, page by page, all of the text of every note that appears in the master PDF file, along with such information as who wrote each note and the date and time it was written. Save the summary file with its own file name.

Archiving

Digital archeology has already begun. If you began working with personal computers in 1986, for example, almost every file you completed that year can no longer be opened. Systems, software, peripherals—all have advanced twentyfold over the past decade. Since the Acrobat Portable Document Format is based on the PostScript language, however, archived PDF files will outlast several iterations of any one creation application. They can be opened, printed, and exchanged, and they can serve as an extractable database of images and text that can be reused or updated.

Once you create a PDF file, use Acrobat Exchange to rearrange pages and move them between different PDF files. If you remove pages from a PDF file, the file retains some information about those deleted pages. The Save As command deletes this extraneous information and reduces the PDF file's size.

Working archives enable you to trace the history of a project's changes. If you consolidate notes in a master PDF file (as explained in "Collating Corrections," page 71), your reviewers' comments are on file permanently. However, you should also set up a final archive—without reviewers' comments—for the approved versions of the project's files.

Working archives. Consider keeping a working archive for each review cycle of a project. If a graphic element was deleted at one cycle and needs to be reincorporated at another, for instance, you can use Adobe Illustrator 5.5 to access the earlier file (see "Extracting Graphics from PDF Files," page 68). Always ask reviewers or clients to return the electronic copy of the PDF file so you can track changes for every review cycle.

Once a review cycle is completed and you have collated corrections in a master PDF file, use the technique detailed in "Disabling Graphics Extraction," page 69, to assign a password and to prevent viewers from altering the archive file.

Final archives. When creating PDF files for final archiving, consider the following suggestions:

- Always embed all fonts used in a document for the final archives. This enables anyone to view that final PDF file later in its most typographically correct form.

- Distill one copy of the final PDF file at low (or no) compression. This allows future users to view the file in its most graphically true form. Distill a second copy at the Distiller default compression settings for everyday use and access from a network server.

- Create thumbnails (in the Distiller Job Options dialog box) when you distill your final PDF file so viewers can preview pages before opening them in Adobe Illustrator 5.5.

Acrobat Search™ and Acrobat Catalog. As your archives grow, the ability to gain access quickly to your PDF files becomes increasingly important. Adobe Acrobat offers a way to perform full-text searches of entire electronic archives in a matter of seconds over a local network or even from remote network locations.

Acrobat Exchange 2.0 includes Acrobat Search, an Acrobat Exchange feature that enables users to conduct full-text searches of anywhere from a few to thousands of PDF files. Acrobat Search reads indexes that are compiled by Acrobat Catalog.

Acrobat Catalog is included with the Acrobat for Workgroups product (and is available separately). Acrobat Catalog compiles a full-text

index of any number of PDF files—even those on gigabyte servers. The program can be set to index the contents of a network server at any time frequency—every week or every night, for instance—and has several options and features for updating and monitoring databases of PDF documents.

When you open Acrobat Search from within Acrobat Exchange (by selecting Tools/Search/Query), you can select index files that have been compiled by Acrobat Catalog. Type in your search query data and select Search. (The Adobe Acrobat Search dialog box contains a full range of search parameters, including Document Info, Date Info, and such options as Word Stemming, Match Case, and Thesaurus. See the user guide for details.)

The Search Results dialog box displays all PDF files that pertain to your query data. Select any of the entries to open that file in Acrobat Exchange.

PDF Archives as a Source of Ideas and Materials

Archives serve multiple purposes when they are digital—and a few more when they are PDF archives. For instance, PDF archives can serve as a visual database of past and present projects.

Archiving on CD-ROM. Your archives don't have to reside on a network server or on optical discs or magnetic tapes locked in a storeroom. Any portion of your PDF archive can easily be loaded onto a master CD-ROM, which can then be manufactured in limited quantities. If you assigned security features to the PDF files, they retain those features when reproduced on the CD-ROM. (You cannot reproduce Adobe Acrobat software on the CD-ROM without first obtaining a license or distribution agreement from Adobe Systems.)

Visual portfolios. You can assemble a visual portfolio of your work from your PDF archives. Using Acrobat Exchange's Insert Pages or Extract Pages feature (under the Edit menu), you can customize a portfolio of any size, even one small enough to fit on a floppy disk.

Customize your PDF portfolio for each client by adding or deleting project examples.

Creating a PDF Presentation Archive

The amount of time that people devote to the creation of presentations and slide shows is amazing. Larger companies devote entire groups of employees to this task, while smaller companies devote huge amounts of their managers' time to creating and re-creating presentations or simply to pulling them together from their paper files (which they must then rekey or re-create). A PDF presentation archive can help meet your presentation demands. The steps for setting up the archive follow.

1. Create a PDF presentation server devoted to all of the presentations your company or department develops. It may be just a folder or directory, either on a server or on your personal computer.

2. Create PDF presentation files the same way you create any PDF file—by "printing" a PostScript file from your creation application and then distilling it. Make sure you select the thumbnails option in the Distiller Job Options dialog box. You might create a Watched Folder on the PDF presentation server to make it easy for coworkers to drop off the PostScript versions of their presentation files for distilling (see "Creating Watched Folders," page 68).

3. Develop a new presentation from existing PDF presentation files by dragging page thumbnails from the thumbnail area of one PDF file to the thumbnail area of another. In doing so, you copy the page and its contents from the first PDF file to the second.

To build a new presentation, first open a PDF presentation file in Acrobat Exchange 2.0, then open an archived PDF presentation file. Display both files in Thumbnails and Page view. Arrange the windows so you can view the two files side-by-side on your monitor by selecting Cascade, Tile Horizontally, or Tile Vertically from the Window menu.

Next, drag thumbnails of archived pages into the thumbnail area of your new presentation file (grab the page number of the thumbnail, not the thumbnail itself). You can rearrange a PDF file's page order in the same way—by moving the thumbnails of the file's pages to the desired sequence. Save the new presentation with a new file name on your personal computer and make a copy for the PDF presentation archive.

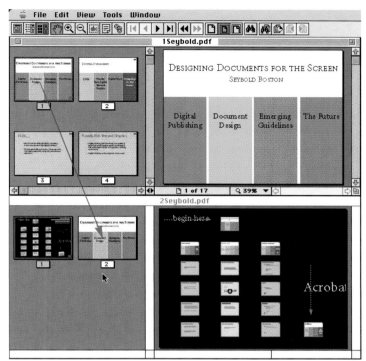

Customize your PDF presentation by dragging thumbnails from one file to another.

Using Full Screen
Acrobat Exchange 2.0 includes a slide-show feature called Full Screen. This option allows Exchange to use the entire monitor screen to display PDF files and to hide all other elements on the monitor. Use Full Screen (in the View menu) to show your portfolio or to make presentations. To cancel the Full Screen view on a Macintosh, press Command-period or the Escape key; with Windows, press the Escape key.

Preparing and Printing Files

Printing: An Overview

Making Color Separations

Setting Flatness for Curves

Trapping Artwork

Printing Files

Understanding Color Bars

Preparing and Printing Files

Your document will print to your expectations most efficiently when you prepare your digital files in advance. Although this preparation requires you to know more about printing than the traditional printing process did, you'll be rewarded with greater control over your work and more reliable results.

This chapter provides information for making color separations in Adobe Photoshop, trapping artwork in Adobe Illustrator, selecting CMY neutrals for quadtones, printing curves more efficiently, working with your prepress vendor, bracketing proofs, and interpreting color bars on a prepress or press proof. Throughout the process, close and clear communication with your prepress and print vendors will prove invaluable.

Printing: An Overview

The most common way to reproduce images and documents is to output a positive or negative image on paper or film and then transfer it to a printing plate to be run on a press. To reproduce continuous-tone images on press, the image is usually broken down into a series of dots. Varying the size or density of the dots creates the optical illusion of variations of gray or color in the image.

In conventional graphics, a halftone image is produced by placing a *halftone screen* between a piece of film and the image and then exposing the film. In the case of four-color printing, four halftone screens are made, one for each ink used in the printing process (the *process colors*): cyan (C), magenta (M), yellow (Y), and black (K). In PostScript production, you specify the attributes for the digital halftone screen prior to producing the film or paper output.

The screen breaks down continuous-tone images, most often into a series of dots that control the amount of ink that is deposited at a specific location. To achieve the best results, the output device you use, such as a PostScript imagesetter, must be mechanically stable and properly calibrated (see Chapter 1, "Working Efficiently"). If these factors are not taken into account, the results will be unpredictable.

Making Color Separations

In four-color reproduction, color separations consist of four pieces of halftone film, one for each process color. The halftones allow the continuous tones of a photographic image or an intricate illustration to be reproduced on a printing press.

Making good color separations is a critical step in preparing your files for print, and mastering the craft requires close communication with your print vendor. Different printing presses, for instance, mix the four process-color inks in slightly different ways, and papers of varying finishes and weights can dramatically affect the appearance of the reproduction. Halftone screens and the dots they produce can sometimes cause problems on press, such as moirés, banding, and dot gain.

STEP-BY-STEP SEPARATIONS USING ADOBE PHOTOSHOP

1. Calibrate your system (use the method described in Chapter 1, "Working Efficiently").

2. Produce the best possible scan (for details, see Chapter 2, "Acquiring Images").

3. Adjust the application's halftone screen, dot-gain, black-ink-generation, and related settings (see "Selecting Your Settings," page 77).

4. Make tonal adjustments and color corrections as desired (see Chapter 3, "Color-Correcting and Editing Images").

5. Convert the RGB image to CMYK (see "Converting to CMYK," page 85) and make final color corrections as needed.

6. Create any necessary trapping (see "Trapping Artwork," page 86).

7. Place the saved image in Adobe Illustrator or a page layout program, if desired.

8. Make digital proofs (see "Printing Files," page 92).

9. Print color separations to paper or film (see "Printing Files," page 92).

10. Make a proof from film.

It's notoriously difficult to match a printed image to the same image shown on a color monitor. The fundamental reason for the difficulty is that each is displayed using a different *color space*—relationships among colors based on a particular color technology. The monitor uses the RGB (red, green, and blue) color space, but the printing press uses the CMY (cyan, magenta, and yellow) color space. Another relevant color space, CIE Lab, is used by Adobe Photoshop to convert images to CMYK mode. (See the user guide for details.)

The capabilities for making color separations are far more extensive in Adobe Photoshop than in Adobe Illustrator because there are more variables to consider in photographic images than in illustrations. This discussion applies primarily to Adobe Photoshop features and capabilities, although in many instances comparable settings can be found in Adobe Separator.™

Working with Your Printer

A reliable print vendor is your best source for information when setting up your files for color separation. Ask your printer these questions so you can work together to produce the best color in a proof and on press:

- What halftone screen frequency (lpi) can the press and plates handle for the level of quality you need? (See "Using Halftone Screen Settings," page 84.)

- What is the expected dot gain in the midtones for the specific paper stock you are using? (See "Compensating for Dot Gain on Press," page 78.)

- Does your print vendor have a preference for using gray component replacement (GCR) or undercolor removal (UCR) to generate the printing plates? (See "Adjusting Black Ink Generation," page 82.)

- What are the total ink and black ink limits of the press? (See "Adjusting Black Ink Generation," page 82.)

- Will you, the printer, or a prepress vendor produce the separated film? (See "Checklist for Working with a Prepress Vendor," page 94.)

Selecting Your Settings

Printing environments vary by press, ink, and paper types as well as by environmental conditions. Making adjustments for the specific printing environment for your project is critical for good color reproduction. Most of these adjustments are made in three Preferences dialog boxes: Monitor Setup, Printing Inks Setup, and Separation Setup. Certain settings, such as halftone screen frequencies, are selected in the Page Setup dialog box and elsewhere.

You should select the appropriate Preferences settings before converting your image to CMYK Color mode. If you convert your image from RGB or Duotone to CMYK Color mode and then change the settings in the Monitor Setup, Printing Inks Setup, and Separation Setup dialog boxes, only the display is affected. For the settings to take effect in the file itself, reopen your original RGB or Duotone file, change the settings, then convert it to CMYK.

Before you begin working in Adobe Photoshop, as part of calibrating your system, use the Adobe Photoshop Gamma control panel or a third-party utility to calibrate your monitor (see Chapter 1, "Working Efficiently," and the user guide). Calibration allows you to eliminate any color cast in your monitor display and to standardize the display of different monitors so that an image is displayed the same regardless of the monitor and video card combination.

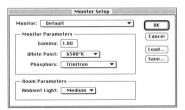

Monitor Setup. In the Monitor Setup dialog box, enter the Gamma setting provided by your calibration utility. Select the Phosphors setting that most closely describes your monitor.

Printing Inks Setup. The options in the Printing Inks Setup dialog box specify the properties of the inks and paper stock you will be using to reproduce your images, as well as the dot gain expected on the final output device. When calibrating your system or preparing files for color separation, you choose the printer type (Ink Colors) you are using; Adobe Photoshop automatically enters dot-gain and gray-balance default values for that printer type. Consult your print vendor for the best settings for your project (see also "Compensating for Dot Gain on Press," page 78).

Changing Modes

Although it's not a good idea to convert between RGB and CMYK modes more than once, the one exception is when the image has been scanned in CMYK mode on a high-end scanner. If the printing environment changes – say, for an advertisement created for a magazine that is now scheduled to run in a newspaper – you may convert the CMYK image to RGB mode, change the settings, then reconvert it to CMYK.

If you are printing files directly from Adobe Photoshop and you are using a PostScript Level 2 color printer, you may want to use the device's built-in Level 2 color separation engine. For best results, specify your monitor and lighting parameters in the Monitor Setup dialog box, then print directly from RGB Color or Lab Color mode.

When you convert to CMYK, record all of your separation settings for that image in the Adobe Photoshop 3.0 File Info dialog box. If you want this information to print with your document, use the Captions attribute in File Info and make sure you check the Caption box in the Page Setup dialog box.

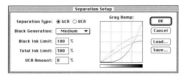

Separation Setup. The Separation Setup settings include the method (GCR or UCR) and degree (for GCR only) of black ink generation; the black ink limit; and the total ink limit for the press. In most cases, the Adobe Photoshop default settings produce excellent results. On the advice of your print vendor, however, you may need to adjust these settings (see also "Adjusting Black Ink Generation," page 82).

Separation Tables. Once you have determined that the settings in the Printing Inks Setup and the Separation Setup dialog boxes produce the colors you want, you can save these settings in a color separation table, naming it for your specific printing device. You can then load the table when separating similar images in the same printing environment. Or you can save several separation tables for the same image, one for each type of printing device you plan to use.

Halftone Screens. Halftone screen attributes include the screen frequency and halftone-dot shape for each screen used in the printing process. For color separations, you may also specify an angle for each of the four halftone screens or have Adobe Photoshop set them automatically (screen-angle and dot-shape settings are best left to experts). Check with your print vendor for the best halftone screen settings to use for your project (see also "Using Halftone Screen Settings," page 84).

Compensating for Dot Gain on Press

Continuous-tone images are reproduced with halftone dots of different sizes—large dots reproduce dark tones and small dots reproduce light tones. During the reproduction process, the dots change in size, usually getting larger. This phenomenon is called *dot gain*. Printed images appear dark and dense unless you compensate for dot gain.

There are many sources of dot gain. Dot gain can occur during plate-making or when the inked plate transfers the image to the rubber blanket on press. The greatest gain, however, occurs when the dot lands on paper—the pressure of the press forces ink into the absorbent paper, which causes the inked halftone dots to spread.

The degree of overall dot gain for a particular press run depends on the printing environment. Individual dot gain depends primarily on the size of dot. The *midtone* (50%) dot has the longest perimeter, and so it increases the most. Small highlight dots grow very little, and since large shadow dots overlap one another, they also show little gain. The accompanying graph shows the typical dot gain from film stage to press-sheet stage plotted against the percentage dot value (representing tone) found on the film. The curve peaks at the 50% tonal value and reaches zero at either end.

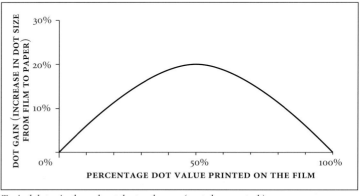

Typical dot gain throughout the tonal range (coated paper stock)

Halftone-dot percentages are measured with a *densitometer*—an instrument for measuring the relative density of any part of an image. A dot-gain percentage value refers to the additive increase and applies only to midtone dots. A 20% dot gain, for instance, means that a 50% midtone dot will print on paper as a 70% dot; it does not mean that a 30% dot (which is not a midtone) will increase to 50%.

Industry surveys of U.S. printers and the SWOP (specifications for web-offset publications) printing standards show a typical dot gain from film stage to press-sheet stage of 18–25% in the midtones when printing on coated stock. Dots grow more on absorbent paper such as uncoated stock, and dot growth is even greater on newsprint. Each of the accompanying illustrations shows, in a magnified section of the same image, the typical dot gain when printing on coated stock, uncoated stock, and newsprint.

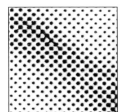 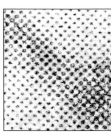 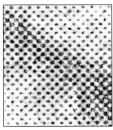

Dot gain on coated stock *Dot gain on uncoated stock* *Dot gain on newsprint*

Adobe Photoshop offers three ways to compensate for dot gain:

1. Setting the dot-gain compensation value in the Printing Inks Setup dialog box.

2. Using the Curves dialog box to compensate manually for dot gain by changing the tonal range in the image.

3. Adjusting Transfer Functions to compensate for dot gain.

There are two ways to compensate for dot gain in grayscale and duotone images: using the Curves dialog box or using Transfer Functions; these images do not benefit from the automatic dot-gain compensation in the Printing Inks Setup dialog box.

Since dot gain is determined by the press, paper, and other reproduction materials, first ask your print vendor for dot-gain specifications for your particular project. Whatever the method, the dot-gain value that Adobe Photoshop needs is the one that occurs between film separation and press sheet.

Using Printing Inks Setup. Whenever you convert an RGB image to CMYK mode, Adobe Photoshop automatically compensates for dot gain. The conversion is optimized for dot-gain values of 20% or more. The value is set in the Printing Inks Setup dialog box.

Always choose the appropriate Ink Colors and Dot Gain settings in Printing Inks Setup prior to converting your image to CMYK or printing comprehensives directly to a digital color printer.

For Ink Colors, choose the description that most closely matches your project—that is, choose SWOP (Newsprint) when printing on newsprint, and so on; Photoshop's default Dot Gain value changes with the Ink Colors setting. The following chart shows default dot-gain values for three SWOP Ink Colors.

INK COLOR SETTING	DEFAULT DOT-GAIN VALUE
SWOP (COATED)	20%
SWOP (UNCOATED)	25%
SWOP (NEWSPRINT)	30%

If you are printing a comprehensive directly to a digital color printer or copier, select the make and model that most closely matches the one you are using; Adobe Photoshop's default Dot Gain value will change accordingly.

If your printer is not listed in the Ink Colors pop-up menu, make a color print or proof of the *Olé No Moiré* file (in the Goodies/Calibration/Separation Sources folder for Photoshop 3.0) from the output device you intend to use. Then hold the print or proof up to the monitor, with the *Olé No Moiré* image displayed on-screen. Determine whether the print matches the on-screen image in intensity. If not, use a different dot-gain value in the Printing Inks Setup dialog box (the CMYK image's display will change but not the file's data). Repeat the process until the two images match. Use the dot-gain value for the matching image as the custom value for that printing device. Whenever you use this printing device in the future, enter this dot-gain value in the Printing Inks Setup dialog box before converting an RGB image to CMYK Color mode (assuming your printing environment hasn't changed).

Using Curves. If you start with a CMYK scan or if you have already converted to CMYK and find that you need to change the amount of dot-gain compensation, you need to compensate for dot gain manually using the Curves dialog box.

With grayscale and duotone images, check the Use Dot Gain for Grayscale Images box in the Printing Inks Setup dialog box. This option changes the image display (but not the image data) to reflect the Dot Gain value in the Printing Inks Setup dialog box. If an image appears too dark after you've checked the grayscale box, compensate for dot gain using the Curves dialog box (this will change your image data to match the image display).

You should calibrate your imagesetter using calibration software from the manufacturer or a third party. If you use a prepress vendor, make sure that the imagesetter is not off by more than two percentage points.

When preparing Adobe Illustrator artwork or working in CMYK Color mode in Adobe Photoshop, you can usually avoid having to adjust for dot gain by choosing colors from a process-color chart printed on the same type of paper (such as coated or uncoated) used for your project. Because the chart is printed, the dot gain for that paper stock is already taken into account, though the color may look incorrect on-screen.

You should also compensate for dot gain manually when you calibrate your system to a certain paper stock—say, coated paper—but go to press with a type of paper that has more dot gain, such as uncoated stock or newsprint. (You can use manual compensation even if you have not calibrated your monitor to a proof.)

In this example, an advertisement is created and placed in a magazine that uses coated stock (Photoshop default dot gain: 20%). Now the same advertisement is scheduled to run in a newspaper (Photoshop default dot gain: 30%), but you want to use the CMYK image because you made some color corrections in CMYK. To compensate manually for the additional dot gain for newsprint after converting to CMYK, choose Image/Adjust/Curves and follow these steps:

1. In the Curves dialog box, display Input and Output values as dot percentages by clicking the bar beneath the curve to toggle their unit of measurement to percentages. In the percentage mode, light Input values (highlights) are on the left of the curve diagram and dark values (shadows) are on the right; light Output values are at the bottom of the diagram and dark values are at the top.

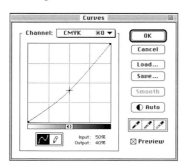

2. With the Channel pop-up menu set to CMYK and the crosshair at the 50% (midtone-dot) level, drag the curve down to the desired Output percentage—in this case, to 40% (for the 10% difference in dot gain)—keeping the Input percentage at 50%.

Consult your printer to find out which percentage dot-gain value will result in a 50% dot when your project is printed on press. You can also compensate for dot gain manually by using Levels (see the *Adobe Photoshop User Guide* for details).

Using Transfer Functions. Another alternative for dot-gain compensation is adjusting the Transfer Functions values (select File/Page Setup/Transfer). Transfer Functions are good for specialized situations such as outputting images for reproduction on newsprint; unlike the Curves method, Transfer Functions do not change the color information in the file.

When saving the Transfer Functions values in an image you intend to export to another application, make sure you save the image in EPS format; then, in the EPS Format dialog box, check the Include Transfer Function box. (See the *Adobe Photoshop User Guide* for more information on Transfer Functions.)

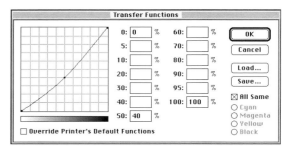

Transfer Functions compensate for dot gain with more precision than other methods.

In most cases, it's best to compensate for dot gain using the settings in Printing Inks Setup or using the Curves (or Levels) dialog box. In all cases, make sure you do not use Transfer Functions with any other dot-gain compensation method; for grayscale and duotone images, do not check the Use Dot Gain for Grayscale Images in the Printing Inks Setup dialog box.

Determining CMY Quadtone Neutrals

The procedure for producing neutral quadtones in Adobe Photoshop is relatively straightforward and can be found in the user guide. Determining which process colors produce neutrals for those quadtones, however, is much more difficult.

Although Photoshop provides preset curves for process-color neutral quadtones (found in the Goodies/Duotone Curves/Quadtones/Process Quadtones folder for Photoshop 3.0), the combinations of CMY that reproduce as neutral are highly specific to the characteristics of each printing environment (press, paper, and ink, for instance). Differences of as little as ±1% in the highlights of any of the three colors and ±2% in the midtones can have a substantial impact on perceived neutrality (see Chapter 3, "Color-Correcting and Editing Images").

Use the chart and instructions on the facing page as a tool for determining which combination of CMY produces a neutral in the printing environment for your project. (This chart can also be used for identifying target values when making tonal adjustments in images, as discussed in Chapter 3.)

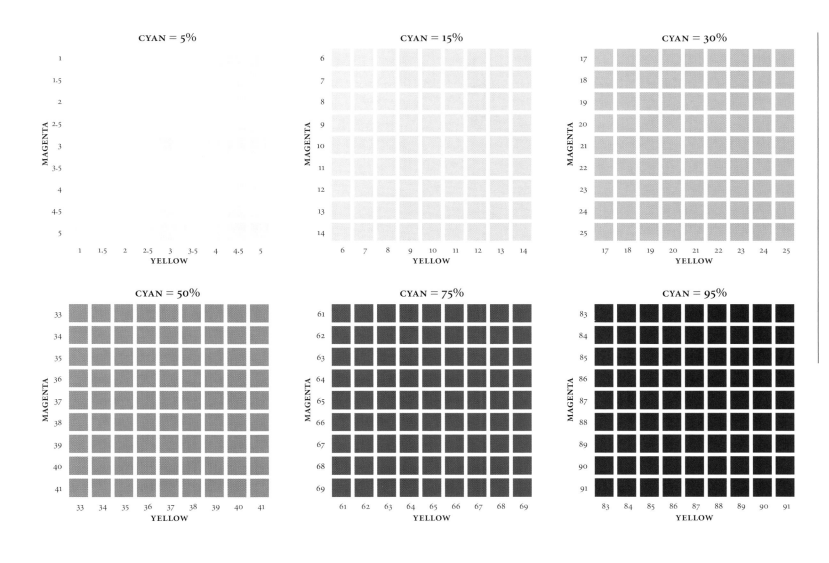

Each of the six matrices contain color swatches having a single value of cyan and varying amounts of magenta and yellow.

Reproduce this chart in Adobe Illustrator and make a color proof or print of it. Cut off the black-only scale beneath the color matrices. Using standardized lighting (see page 96), compare the color swatches in your proof with the elements in the black-only scale.

You should find six combinations of CMY – one from each matrix – that produce neutrals in your printing environment.

CUT PROOF HERE   CUT PROOF HERE

5 8 11 14 17 20 23 26 29 32 35 38 41 44 47 50 53 56 59 62 65 68 71 74 77 80 83 86 89 92 95

This chart is based on the Tone Reproduction and Neutral Determination (TRAND) concept.

GCR and UCR

With the GCR method, black ink replacement occurs throughout the image. GCR separations help maintain gray balance (the mix of CMY required to produce a neutral) on press and lower printing costs (black ink is less expensive than CMY inks). Consult your printer to determine which method to use.

With UCR, the neutral produced by CMY inks is replaced by black only in the shadow areas, which enhances details.

Also shown on this page are the Gray Ramp graphs (found in the Separation Setup dialog box) associated with the two groups of images. The Gray Ramp graph shows how the neutrals in the image will separate under the Separation Setup parameters. In this example, the only difference in the two sets of parameters is the switch from GCR to UCR.

Adjusting Black Ink Generation

In theory, cyan, magenta, and yellow (CMY) inks produce a pure black when combined in equal amounts; in practice, however, ink impurities often make the color a muddy brown. So black ink (K) is added to ensure good reproduction of an image.

When black ink is added to the other process colors, however, the combined inks can become too thick, causing smudging and drying problems on press. The amounts of black ink and combined inks that can be accommodated vary from one press to another. In addition, with black ink added it's not necessary to use 100% strengths of CMY inks, which are more expensive than black ink, to create dense shadow areas. The two most common techniques for removing the excess CMY inks are *gray component replacement* (GCR) and *undercolor removal* (UCR), both of which are found in the Adobe Photoshop Separation Setup dialog box.

The images on this page show the effects of GCR and UCR on an image; the images on the facing page show the effects of changes in the Total Ink Limit value, which is also found in the Separation Setup dialog box.

GCR: CMYK composite

GCR: black plate

GCR: CMY plates

UCR: CMYK composite

UCR: black plate

UCR: CMY plates

TOTAL INK LIMIT: 240

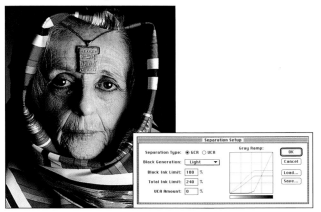

CMYK composite

Cyan plate

Magenta plate

Yellow plate

Black plate

TOTAL INK LIMIT: 320

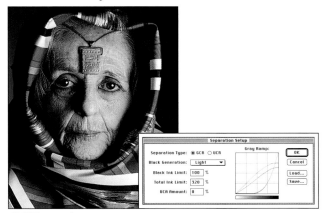

CMYK composite

Cyan plate

Magenta plate

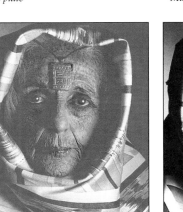

Yellow plate

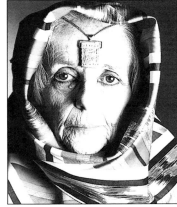

Black plate

Total Ink Limit

The effects of changes in total ink limit on a selected image are displayed here. As the Total Ink Limit value increases (with all other settings remaining constant), the black ink is replaced by the more subtle neutral of the CMY inks. The composites, however, show only a subtle change in the image. Consult your print vendor for the Total Ink Limit value, which is the maximum ink density that your press can support.

Producing a Color Comprehensive

At times you may need to produce a color comprehensive using different color separation settings than you need on press. In this case, make a copy of the original RGB file, change your settings in the Printing Inks Setup dialog box to match the requirements of the proofing device you will use for the comp, then convert the file to CMYK Color mode and print. Make any further changes in the original RGB file; when you are ready for film output, reset your Printing Inks Setup for press requirements, convert to CMYK, and output your film.

Using Halftone Screen Settings

Adobe Photoshop provides several options for selecting halftone screen attributes, which are found in the Halftone Screens dialog box (File/Page Setup/Screen). You can select all attributes yourself on advice from your print vendor, though screen-angle and dot-shape settings are best left to experts. To set the screen frequencies and angles for the four process-color halftone screens automatically in Adobe Photoshop, click the Auto button and enter the resolution of the output device and the screen frequency you intend to use in the Auto Screens dialog box.

If you are placing Adobe Photoshop images in a page layout program, select your halftone screen frequencies once in the page layout application rather than for each image in Photoshop. Photoshop screen frequencies can be saved for export only in EPS format, and then only when the Include Halftone Screens box is checked in the EPS Format dialog box. More importantly, if any Photoshop image's screen frequency conflicts with that of the page layout program or output device, the conflict could produce undesired results when the file is printed, depending on which settings—those of Photoshop, the page layout program, or the printing device—override the others.

Another way to specify halftone screen frequencies is to check the Use Printer's Default Screens box in the Halftone Screens dialog box. The specifications from the Halftone Screens dialog box are then shaded and are not applicable when the screens are generated during output. (If you check the Use Printer's Default Screens box and print directly from Photoshop, the printer's default screen frequency is used.)

Certain setting combinations result in the Photoshop default screen frequency of 53 lpi, which then overrides the frequency of any page layout or graphics application in which the images are placed.

There are three key settings in the six versions of the image shown on this page; all other settings remain constant. The only combination that results in the 53-lpi default setting is when the Use Printer's Default Screens box is not checked, the Include Halftone Screens box (shown when you save in EPS format) is checked, and the Photoshop default screen frequency is not changed.

The best way to ensure that you do not get the 53-lpi screen frequency in error is to leave both the Use Printer's Default Screens and the Include Halftone Screens boxes unchecked and set your screen frequency in the page layout or graphics program.

COMBINATIONS OF HALFTONE SCREEN SETTINGS (PAGE LAYOUT APPLICATION LPI: 150)

☐ INCLUDE HALFTONE SCREENS   ☒ INCLUDE HALFTONE SCREENS   ☒ INCLUDE HALFTONE SCREENS

☐ USE PRINTER'S DEFAULT SCREENS

Photoshop lpi: 53
Photoshop settings are not saved

Photoshop lpi: 53
Photoshop overrides page layout

Photoshop lpi: 150
Photoshop overrides page layout

☒ USE PRINTER'S DEFAULT SCREENS

Photoshop lpi: N/A
Page layout settings prevail

Photoshop lpi: N/A
Page layout settings prevail

Photoshop lpi: N/A
Page layout settings prevail

Converting to CMYK

When you convert an RGB image to CMYK mode for color separation, Adobe Photoshop uses its color separation utility to transform the RGB colors into the four process colors. Color values may shift slightly as pixels are altered each time the image is converted, so it's best not to convert between RGB and CMYK mode more than once. And because certain settings take effect only when a file is converted to CMYK, work with a copy of your RGB file, not the original, in case you need to convert the original later with new settings (see "Selecting Your Settings," page 77).

CIE Lab is a large, device-independent color space that includes all six primary colors (red, green, blue, cyan, magenta, and yellow) in the RGB and CMY color spaces. Thus, it serves as an accurate intermediate mode for color conversion. The goal of Adobe Photoshop in converting RGB images is to match the printed CMYK results to what the user is likely to see on the monitor. In a process transparent to the user, Adobe Photoshop first converts the RGB color values to Lab color values using the information in the Monitor Setup dialog box. It then uses the settings in the Printing Inks Setup and Separation Setup dialog boxes to build a color separation table based on the image's Lab color values. Photoshop uses these Lab color values to build an equivalent CMYK separation table (see the user guide for more details).

Separating Adobe Illustrator Files

Adobe Separator is required to generate color separations from Adobe Illustrator files that are not placed in a page layout program. Before a prepress vendor can print color separations from the Adobe Separator program, however, the file must be saved with Adobe Illustrator in Encapsulated PostScript (EPS) format. Adobe Separator may not correctly print separations of a file saved in another application, even if the file was saved in EPS format.

After opening Adobe Separator, the prepress vendor opens the artwork and PostScript Printer Description files, places any requested crop marks and bleed around the artwork, sets the separation options specified by the print vendor, and saves the file for separation.

To overprint black or to print more than one custom color on the same press plate, open the Separations dialog box, then hold down the Option key while choosing either Print Selected Separations or Save Selected Separations from the File menu. Click Yes as needed when two successive alerts ask whether you want these options. The *Adobe Illustrator User Guide* provides thorough instructions on how to use Adobe Separator.

Setting Flatness for Curves

PostScript interpreters approximate curves by a series of line segments. If the line segments are short enough, the individual line segments will not be visible and the curve will appear smooth. A raster image processor (RIP) calculates a series of short line segments more quickly and easily than it does a perfect curve. The trade-off, then, is between an output device's rendering accuracy and its calculation time.

The PostScript page description language allows some variance in the way an output device renders curves. The level of accuracy in a curve rendering is determined in part by the user's adjustment of the flatness value. The *flatness value* represents the amount, in pixels, by which a particular curve rendering varies from a perfect rendering. You can adjust this value for complex curves in Adobe Illustrator; in Adobe Photoshop, flatness is used only when you save a clipping path to silhouette an image and place it in other applications.

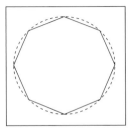

If the flatness value is set too high, a circle will be made up of lengthy line segments rather than curves, resulting in a polygon instead of a circle. But if the flatness value is set too low, the RIP may have to make many more calculations than are necessary to produce a good-looking curve, resulting in unnecessarily lengthy output times.

Although a straight line is not affected by the flatness value, curves are affected in ways that are difficult to predict and depend upon the resolution of the output device. A flatness value of 25, for instance, may produce angular and sharp-edged output on a 300-dpi laser printer but quite acceptable output on a 3386-dpi imagesetter.

On the other hand, your file may print trouble-free on a 300-dpi laser printer but not on a high-resolution imagesetter (in this case, you would increase the flatness value). The trick is to find a flatness value that works well at the printing device's resolution.

Setting flatness in Adobe Illustrator. Rather than changing the flatness value directly, in Adobe Illustrator you instead change the output resolution according to the following formula:

$$\text{FLATNESS} = \frac{\text{PRINTING DEVICE RESOLUTION}}{\text{OUTPUT DEVICE RESOLUTION}}$$

While in RGB mode in Adobe Photoshop 3.0, choose CMYK Preview from the Mode menu. This feature lets you preview, prior to making the actual conversion, how the RGB image is likely to look both in CMYK Color mode and when printed to the device specified in the Printing Inks Setup dialog box.

If your artwork contains very long or complex curved paths, you may want to change the flatness value by changing the Adobe Illustrator default Output Resolution setting of 800 dpi. Set the output resolution for all new objects (but not existing objects) in the Document Setup dialog box; for individual existing objects, select the object, then set its Output Resolution value in the Objects/Attributes dialog box. Output Resolution settings must be between 100 dpi and 9600 dpi in Illustrator 5.0 and later versions. Flatness can also be adjusted using an Adobe Illustrator EPSF Riders file (see "EPSF Riders Files," page 93).

Setting flatness in Adobe Photoshop. Flatness values in Adobe Photoshop come into play when you use clipping paths. A *clipping path* is a path drawn with the pen tool and saved with the document in EPS format; it makes everything but the selected area transparent when the image is printed or previewed in another application.

The flatness value for clipping paths is set in the Clipping Path dialog box after you save a clipping path, or it is set in the EPS Format dialog box when you save the file in EPS format (see the user guide for details). Values can range from 0.2 to 100; if you do not enter a value, Adobe Photoshop uses the printer's default setting. In general, a flatness value of 8–10 is recommended for high-resolution printing devices (1200–2400 dpi), and a setting of 1–3 is recommended for low-resolution printing devices (300–600 dpi).

Trapping Artwork

In offset printing, paper can shift slightly, causing small but unsightly gaps where different-colored elements meet. Traditionally, print vendors compensated for this *misregistration* in advance by creating a small area of overlap (called *trapping*) between two adjoining colors.

In digital prepress, traps are created by using the more sophisticated graphics, page layout, and trapping programs. In Adobe Illustrator, for instance, traps are created by selecting some elements in the artwork to *overprint* others, which results in both inks overlapping and a transparent appearance on press. Since the trap amount varies with press and paper types, it's important to consult your printer to determine how much trapping to apply to any particular image.

Two types of traps can be created digitally: *spread traps,* in which the object's edge is extended and overprints (overlaps) the background; and *choke traps,* in which the background's adjoining edge is extended and overprints the object.

Trapping with Adobe Photoshop
Misregistration is less likely to be visible with photographic images because the process-color dots intermingle throughout the image. If any distinctly different colors in your image touch, however, you may need to trap. Consult your printer to find out how much trapping is appropriate for your project (the trap amount varies with image resolution; that is, a 1-pixel trap width is much more obvious in a 72-ppi image than in a 300-ppi image).

1. Open a copy of the RGB or CMYK image that you want to trap. Convert an RGB image to CMYK mode (the Adobe Photoshop Trap feature works only in CMYK mode).

2. Make a selection, if desired. Here, we selected an area where a green leaf and red berry meet; they have distinctly different colors, which could be a source of misregistration on press.

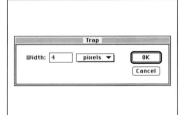

3. Choose Image/Trap; the Trap dialog box appears. Choose a unit of measurement from the pop-up menu. Enter the trap width in the Width box; click OK.

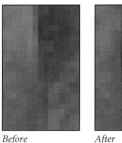

Before   *After*

4. Photoshop creates allover traps within the selection. In these magnified before-and-after views, you can see the effects of the Trap feature on the selection.

Trapping with Adobe Illustrator

Adobe Illustrator has extensive trapping capabilities, including the Pathfinder Trap filter plug-in in version 5.5. The complexity of your artwork will determine which method you use. As with the Adobe Photoshop Trap feature, the Illustrator trap filter uses one method among many for trapping and thus is intended to be used with uncomplicated artwork. For example, it works well with simple graphics and type, but if your artwork has gradients, strokes, or other complex elements, you should trap manually.

Analyze the trapping needs of your document before trapping; Illustrator does not trap patterns, for instance. Use the Pathfinder Trap filter when trapping fewer than twenty-five overlapping shapes filled with process and custom colors. Use manual trapping for objects containing fills, text, strokes, or placed images; the Pathfinder Trap filter will ignore these attributes.

Consult with your prepress and press vendors for their trapping requirements before using the trap filter. If you aren't sure about how to create specific traps for your artwork, consider having your prepress vendor's staff produce traps for you. (See the *Adobe Illustrator User Guide* for more information on trapping.)

The Pathfinder Trap filter. This plug-in compares the two objects you want to trap, then selects the lighter object to overprint (trap) the darker one. If two objects are similar in color density, the Pathfinder Trap filter selects one based on subtle color variations. If you are not satisfied with the results—for instance, if overprinting a blue object on a red background results in a distinctly purple outline—you can use the Reverse Trap option in the Pathfinder Trap dialog box (select Filter/Pathfinder/Trap) to select the other object for overprinting.

The Pathfinder Trap filter works best when you select only two objects at a time. Be sure you have deselected all other objects before applying the trap filter; when too many objects are selected, the trap filter takes a long time to process.

Generally, it is best to scale your graphic to the finished size before you use the trap filter because the trap amount you specify increases or decreases proportionally when you change the scale of the object. If you create a graphic that has 0.5-point traps and scale it to five times its original size, for example, the result will be 2.5-point traps for the enlarged graphic.

Trapping manually. The manual trapping method offers far more flexibility than the Pathfinder Trap filter. Spread and choke traps are both available, and you (rather than the program) select which object will overprint another.

Manual trapping is an art; not only must the printer and paper types be considered, but also whether the objects share ink colors, whether they contain gradients or continuous-tone images, and whether any blacks are actually a mixture of process colors. Pages 88–92 show trapping approaches for these and other complexities in an image.

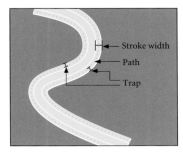

Because a stroke in the Adobe Illustrator program "straddles" a boundary—that is, half of the stroke is on one side of the boundary, and half on the other—you should use a stroke that's double the trap width recommended by your printer.

Most approaches make use of the Overprint option in the Paint Style palette, which causes the affected printing inks to overlap on press. To create basic 1-point spread traps for a yellow object on a blue background, for instance, you would create a 2-point yellow stroke for the object and set the stroke to overprint the background.

Since the object itself is not set to Overprint, the blue background drops out ("knocks out") beneath it. Because the stroke straddles the object's boundary, only the outer 1 point overprints the background, creating the appropriate amount of trap.

In general, misregistration is less noticeable when adjacent objects share at least one color. Whenever one object is black, you can introduce shared colors by converting the black to a two- or four-color black (black plus either one or three process colors). The multicolor black is also much richer than 100% black alone, and two-color blacks are easier than four-color blacks to register on press.

100% black   *Two-color black*   *Four-color black*

Spread or Choke?

For best results, you should trap (overprint) the lighter area into the darker area. For example, if the background is darker than the foreground, you would use spread traps (the lighter object overprints and "spreads" into the darker background). If the background is lighter than the foreground, you would use choke traps (the lighter background overprints and "chokes" the darker object).

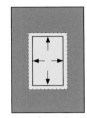
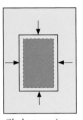

Spread trapping   *Choke trapping*

Manual Trapping

Manual trapping is a subjective process in which there are no set rules, so two very different approaches may work equally well on the same artwork.

The following pages show the techniques that were applied to the complex trapping problems in two illustrations – the first created with both Adobe Illustrator and Adobe Photoshop and the second created in Adobe Illustrator alone.

All trapping is created using Adobe Illustrator.

Trapping Backgrounds to Photographic Images

1. To trap masks used to frame placed EPS images on a background, open the Layers palette, then choose New Layer in the pop-up menu. Name the new layer Trap. Select a color from the Selection Color pop-up menu that is different from the mask color in the artwork layer; click OK.

2. Select all masks on the artwork layer that need trapping, then copy (⌘C) and select Paste In Front (⌘F). To move the copied masks to the Trap layer, click on the small colored square to the right of the artwork layer in the Layers palette and drag it up to the Trap layer. Hide the artwork layer by clicking the dot beneath the eye icon in the Layers palette. If any masks overlap (as in this example), apply the Unite filter (Filter/Pathfinder/Unite).

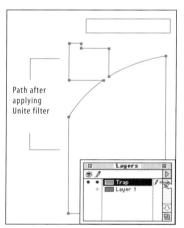

3. Stroke the trap shapes using the background color; make the stroke widths double your trap width and set the strokes to Overprint. These strokes are your traps. Click on the space beneath the eye icon in the Layers palette to see the entire artwork again.

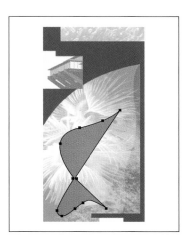

Trapping Gradients
On Grayscale Images

1. Gradients on grayscale images present a difficult trapping problem because strokes cannot be filled with gradients. This technique creates trapping using a slightly smaller copy of the gradient object. Select the gradient object that needs trapping.

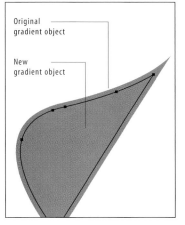

Original gradient object

New gradient object

2. To create the copy, choose the Offset Path filter (Filter/Objects/ Offset Path). In the Offset Path dialog box, enter the trap width as a negative number in the Offset box. Click OK.

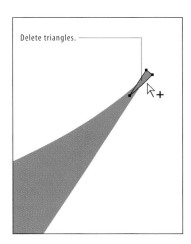

Delete triangles.

3. If your shape has corners, the path created by the Offset Path filter has triangle shapes at each corner. With the new gradient object still selected, choose the Exclude filter (Filter/Pathfinder/ Exclude), which separates the triangle paths from the rest of the path. Deselect. Using the direct-selection tool, hold down the Option key, select just the triangle, and delete it.

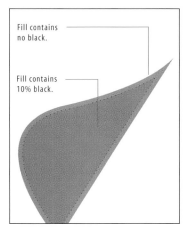

Fill contains no black.

Fill contains 10% black.

4. If your gradient has black in it, as ours does, the black must be removed from the original bottom object or it cannot overprint on the black plate. Select the Gradient dialog box (Object/ Gradient), then your object's gradient. Click on the Duplicate button, then remove black from the new gradient. Select the original gradient object and fill with the new gradient. Set only the bottom object to Overprint.

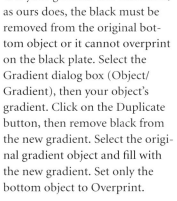

Top stroke: 2.8 points Set to Overprint

Bottom stroke: 2.5 points

Trapping Strokes

To trap strokes, copy the stroke and choose Paste In Front (⌘F). Widen the top stroke width by double the trap width. Set the top stroke to Overprint; leave the Overprint box for the bottom stroke unchecked so it knocks out the background.

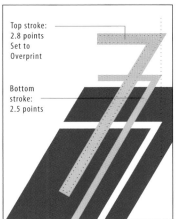

Set to Overprint

date: july 15 – 25

place: marine life research

subject: underwater climate and its relationship to marine life forms

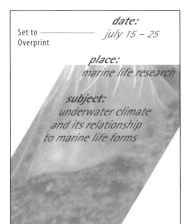

Trapping Small Type
And Thin Rules

When type is small and darker than the background, as ours is, leave all type untrapped but set it to Overprint.

Use the same method for thin rules such as the red and black rules in this example. Since they are too thin to trap, simply set them to Overprint.

⊕ Regardless of your trapping method, always consult your print vendor for the correct trap width to use early in the process. Then build traps into the file as you work.

⊕ Trapping is not necessary where two continuous-tone images meet – in this artwork, one is grayscale and one a four-color image. There are enough common colors in both (here, in the black plate) that any misregistration is unlikely to show.

Consider using layers to separate trapped objects (including stroke traps) from the objects themselves. You can then use the Layers options to simplify subsequent editing and retrapping.

Create traps on a copy of your file, not the original, so you can start fresh if your first trapping approach doesn't work for you.

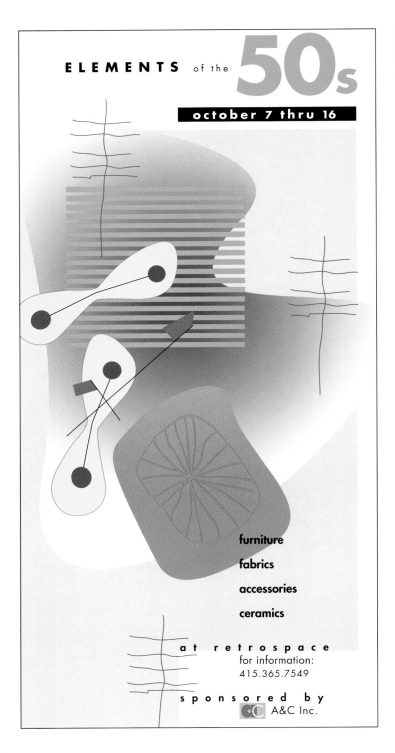

Trapping Backgrounds to Foreground Elements

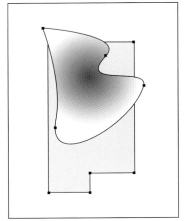

1. When a tint background and a foreground object have no common colors, misregistration can occur on press. To trap the background and the object, select and copy both (⌘C), then choose Paste In Front (⌘F).

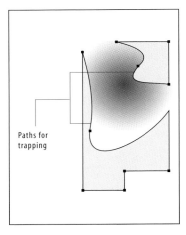

Paths for trapping

2. Isolate the background by choosing the Minus Front filter (under Filter/Pathfinder). This filter creates paths for trapping.

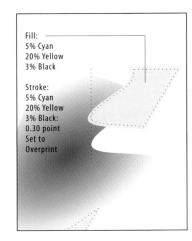

Fill:
5% Cyan
20% Yellow
3% Black

Stroke:
5% Cyan
20% Yellow
3% Black:
0.30 point
Set to
Overprint

3. To create traps for the new paths, add strokes that are double your trap width and the same color as the background.

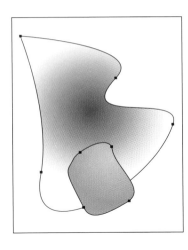

Trapping Gradients On Gradients

1. Gradients with no common colors are one of the most difficult to trap. It is critical that you first consult with your prepress vendor to determine which gradient will hold the trapping (call this the "host object"). Then open a copy of your file (not the original) and select both objects. Choose Copy (⌘C), then Paste In Front (⌘F). Deselect.

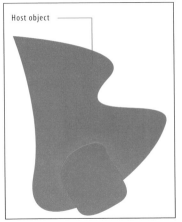

Host object

2. Select the copy of the host object (here, the purple radial; see also step 1) and fill it with 100% magenta. Select the copy of the other gradient object and fill it with 100% cyan. (These flat-color fills will be eliminated in later steps.)

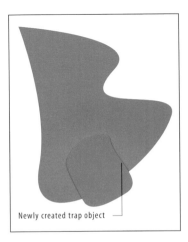

Newly created trap object

3. Select both flat-color objects and apply the trap filter (Filter/ Pathfinder/Trap). The resulting shape is your "trap object." The trap object overlays the magenta object, which is on top of the host object.

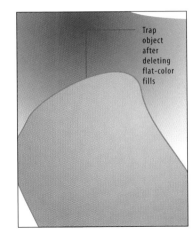

Trap object after deleting flat-color fills

4. Select the original flat-color objects and delete them, leaving only the two original gradients and the trap object. The trap filter automatically sets the trap object to Overprint.

5. To make a gradient with colors common to both original gradients, open the Gradient dialog box (Object/Gradient). Select the gradient used in the host object (we've used White & Purple Radial), then click on the Duplicate button to create a copy. Add some of one color in the other gradient to the new gradient (here, we've added 35% yellow). Save your file.

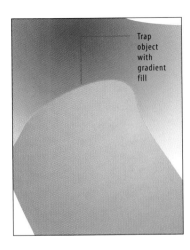

Trap object with gradient fill

6. Select the trap object, then fill it with the new gradient. To align the gradient of the trap object closely to that of the host object, select only the trap object, not the host object. Choose the gradient fill tool and drag it from the host object through the trap object. Experiment with different vectors and colors until the two gradients align and blend well. (See also "Aligning Trap Gradients.")

Aligning Trap Gradients

When trapping two gradients, it is very important to align the trap object's gradient and that of the object beneath (call this the "host object"). It is best to align the two gradients precisely, but slight misalignments should not affect small traps.

Exact alignments can be created for both linear and radial gradients. When linear gradients have not been manipulated using the gradient fill tool, select the host object and note the value of its gradient in the Angle box (found in the Paint Style dialog box). Select the trap object and enter the same value in its Angle box; press Return. The gradients of both objects align exactly.

Precise alignment of radial gradients are more difficult because they do not have angles. This method uses the gradient fill tool, which complicates matters because it changes the original artwork. Work on a copy of your artwork, not the original. Select both objects. Choose the gradient fill tool and drag it from the host object across the trap object. The two gradients align.

To reduce printing problems, limit the complexity of patterns, masks, and compound paths as well as the number of downloadable typefaces in the artwork file.

When drawing freehand or using the autotrace tool in Adobe Illustrator, you can simplify paths by increasing the Freehand Tolerance value or the Auto Trace Gap distance in the General Preferences dialog box (in the File menu) before you create a path. A higher value or distance decreases the number of points on a path and thus decreases memory requirements.

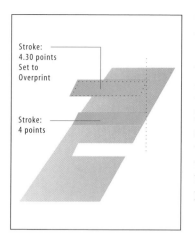

Stroke:
4.30 points
Set to
Overprint

Stroke:
4 points

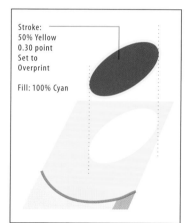

Stroke:
50% Yellow
0.30 point
Set to
Overprint

Fill: 100% Cyan

The Pathfinder
Trap filter
creates trapping
automatically.

Trapping Strokes

The orange pattern is made up of individual strokes (Adobe Illustrator does not trap patterns). Select and copy (⌘C) all strokes, then choose Paste In Front (⌘F). Make the width of all top strokes slightly larger than the originals, then set to Overprint. For the bottom strokes, leave the Overprint box unchecked so the background knocks out.

Trapping Solid-Color Objects

Solid-color objects, such as this blue circle on yellow, are simple to trap. Select the top object, then add a thin yellow stroke set to Overprint. The stroke traps the blue circles in the yellow shapes.

Trapping for the two red "flags" and the irregular red "wheel" is accomplished in a similar manner—by adding thin red strokes set to Overprint to each object or border.

Using the Pathfinder Trap Filter

Use the Pathfinder Trap filter to create automatic traps for simple artwork elements such as this company logo. Select two shapes at a time to trap (in this example, the letter *a* and the background). Choose the trap filter (Filter/ Pathfinder/Trap). Repeat the process until all your elements are trapped.

Printing Files

Your project files will print more efficiently if you understand how to work with your prepress vendor. Along with helping you achieve this goal, this section includes techniques for proofing economically and an introduction to the familiar but mysterious color bars found on most prepress and press proofs.

Selecting the Right Proofing Device

With the wide range of digital proofing devices now available, it's important to recognize the distinctions among them so you can choose the device most appropriate for your project. A color laser copier may serve you well for rough color proofs, for instance, but your print vendor will not accept its output as a *contract proof*—that is, a proof the vendor is contractually liable to match. Then again, color laser copier output lets you know early—and inexpensively— whether your design is on the right color track. Make sure your device supports the PostScript language.

Bracketing Proofs

You can use Adobe Photoshop 3.0 or Adobe Illustrator to print two or more versions of the same photographic image on the same proof sheet. This concept is called *bracketing* and is based on techniques used in photography (see also Chapter 3, "Color-Correcting and Editing Images").

You can use this versatile method to proof two sets of color corrections, two CMYK translations of custom colors, two sets of contrast adjustments in a grayscale image, or other variations in your image.

The Photoshop technique takes up less hard disk space and results in a full-size image split in two; with the Illustrator technique, each image is whole (unsplit), but you may have to reduce the image sizes to fit them on one proof sheet. Both methods reduce proofing costs.

Bracketing with Adobe Illustrator. Bracketing with Adobe Illustrator is straightforward: Save two or more Adobe Photoshop images with different color or Preferences settings in EPS format, place them in Illustrator, then produce film and a proof (see "Separating Adobe Illustrator Files," page 85).

Bracketing with Adobe Photoshop 3.0. The Adobe Photoshop 3.0 method works with images in CMYK and Grayscale modes, though not in Duotone mode. The following example produces a single proof showing two variations of color corrections in the same image.

1. Open your original file. Choose Save As and add the suffix *.original* to the end of the file name (in Windows, limit suffixes to three letters—*.org*, for instance).

2. Choose Image/Duplicate. In the Duplicate Image dialog box, rename the suffix (here, we've used *.corrected* since we are color-correcting this image). Click OK.

3. Without changing the duplicate image's dimensions or resolution, make your adjustments (here, we've brightened the image using Curves). Save the file (⌘S) without changing its name. The *.original* and the *.corrected* files are the two you'll be bracketing.

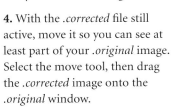

4. With the *.corrected* file still active, move it so you can see at least part of your *.original* image. Select the move tool, then drag the *.corrected* image onto the *.original* window.

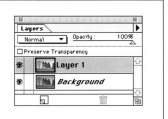

5. Close the *.corrected* window. Open the Layers palette (Window/ Palettes/Show Layers) in the *.original* file; the *.corrected* image appears as Layer 1.

6. Select Layer 1 in the Layers palette, then choose Add Layer Mask from the pop-up menu. The layer mask appears next to the image in Layer 1.

7. With the layer mask still selected, make a selection (we chose the right half).

8. Make sure the foreground color is black and use it to fill the selection (Option-Delete). The *.original* image shows through the filled area. Deselect (⌘D); choose Save As and use the suffix *.bracket*. The image is now split and ready for proofing.

9. To print a composite, make sure the eye icons are on in both Layer 1 and the Background layer, then print. To print film and a proof of the split image, select Flatten Image in the Layers pop-up menu, then print.

EPSF Riders Files

You create an Adobe Illustrator EPSF Riders file with the Make Riders filter (select Filter/Other/ Make Riders); it allows you to modify, using PostScript language code, the halftone screen frequency and angle, flatness, and other settings at print time.

Because all files that are saved as EPS files or printed from Illustrator are affected once an Adobe Illustrator EPSF Riders file is created, you may wish to remove the Riders information from your files so they will print more efficiently.

To remove the Adobe Illustrator EPSF Riders file from your system, use the Delete Riders filter (select Filter/Other/Delete Riders). Then restart Adobe Illustrator and resave all documents that contain embedded Riders information.

Printing Patterns

The time it takes your pattern to preview and print depends on the pattern's complexity and on the memory available in your system and in your printer. Simple patterns print the fastest. A printer may slow or stall in printing a pattern if the printer's memory is full or if the pattern is too large for the memory. If your pattern takes a long time to print or if it won't print at all, consider simplifying the pattern or the shape it fills. Also, before creating a pattern from a complex drawing, remove any detail that is too small to appear in your final printed output. Avoid both filling and stroking a shape with a pattern whenever possible. Delete all unused patterns from your artwork. If the artwork uses several patterns, keep them simple.

Checklist for Working with a Prepress Vendor

Just as in the conventional prepress process, you can minimize surprises and surcharges from your digital prepress vendor by following your prepress vendor's recommendations and by submitting clean and complete files and associated information. Use the following checklist when preparing your files for the prepress vendor.

☐ **Create a label.** If your application doesn't provide automatic labels, create a ❶ label in your file that will print at least the file name and date.

☐ **Eliminate unnecessary elements.** Delete all extraneous colors, patterns, and other elements from the file, including those that may be invisible or behind other elements or layers.

☐ **Use the correct format.** Make sure all files are in the correct format. Consult your prepress vendor for the best format to use.

☐ **Set halftone screens correctly.** If you plan to place Adobe Photoshop images saved in EPS format in a page layout document, select your ❷ halftone screen frequency in the page layout program rather than in each image. If any image screen frequency conflicts with that of the page layout application, the image setting may override that of the document, often with unpleasant results.

☐ **Size and rotate art.** As much as possible, provide ❸ sized art in the correct rotated position to the prepress vendor. Sizing, cropping, and rotating raster images (such as Adobe Photoshop images) in a page layout application are very complex operations; as a result, the raster image processor (RIP) may take a long time to process the file.

☐ **Make spot colors consistent.** If you use the same ❹ spot color and tint several times in one document, make sure each object's process or custom color and tint, as well as its name, is identical to the others. Indicate whether you want the vendor to convert the custom colors to process colors.

☐ **List document elements.** Use the Adobe Illustrator 5.5 Document Info filter (Filter/Other/Document Info) to create a list of custom colors, fonts, patterns, placed art, and other items used in your document; include a printout with your output file.

☐ **Record separation settings.** Use the Adobe Photoshop 3.0 File Info feature (in the File menu) to record the separation settings you used when converting your image to CMYK. To print this information when proofing your image, use the Captions attribute in File Info, then check the Caption box in the Page Setup dialog box.

☐ **Provide laser prints.** Print your files first on a PostScript laser printer. Send ❺ laser prints with your files—making sure they are identical to the files—so the prepress vendor can check against them.

☐ **Group graphics and document files.** Copy all of the graphics required for your files and place them in the same folder or directory as the page layout or other output files. Make sure the same versions of all images are linked to their correct placements in the document.

☐ **Provide contact information.** In a work order or cover letter, list your name, company name, and contact names and phone numbers, including after-hours numbers, if applicable.

☐ **Include document specifications.** List each file name, document page size, number of pages, which pages to print from each file, and the type of output you need.

☐ **Identify your film requirements.** For each output file, indicate whether you want a positive or negative, the emulsion direction, and the screen frequency for film output.

☐ **List font file names.** Provide the precise file names and manufacturers of every typestyle of every ❻ font used in your document, as well as whether each is a Type 1 or TrueType font.

☐ **Indicate your trapping needs.** For color separations, indicate whether you've created ❼ trapping yourself or want the prepress vendor to do it (usually for a fee).

☐ **Take responsibility.** If the prepress vendor rather than the print vendor is producing separated film, it is your responsibility to ensure that all parties are in agreement about the requirements of the print job.

☐ **Inform your vendor.** Convey any other special instructions that apply, such as whether the graphics are intended to be for position only.

Japan

Traditional
Kamakura, a short train ride from Tokyo, is rich with cultural history and home to the second largest Buddha in Japan.

Contemporary
Walking the verdant grounds of the Hakone Sculpture Garden is at once peaceful and stimulating.

Traditional

contemporary

Authentic
Come 4 a.m., Tsukiji, Tokyo's bustling fish market, is the wildest show in town. Sit in on the tuna auction or sample the squid; it's well worth losing some sleep over.

But Japanese cuisine isn't just raw fish. It's a precise palette of tastes and textures to be savored and enjoyed by the eyes as well as the tongue.

48 · 49

If your prepress vendor does not have the latest version of Adobe Illustrator, use the latest version to save a copy of the document in EPS format. Then it can be placed into an earlier version of Illustrator or into another desktop publishing program without losing any of the document's printing enhancements or tabs.

Before outputting rough proofs on a laser printer, you can minimize PostScript errors by first making sure that the settings in the Page Setup dialog box are correct for your printer.

Standard Lighting

If you expect to get predictable results from your color reproduction system, you must consider the lighting where you work and the lighting you use to check proofs.

In a truly professional working environment, you'll find workstations in rooms with no windows; walls painted neutral gray; consistent, color-correct (5000° Kelvin) lighting; monitors calibrated to the final color output; and viewing booths with color-correct lighting.

Since most of us don't have such a workplace, you should try to maintain consistent lighting in your work area. If your computer is near a window, cover the window so that the light on your monitor is as consistent as possible. View proofs in color-correct light. If you have to look at proofs without the benefit of color-correct light, always view all your proofs under the same lighting conditions.

Understanding Color Bars

Color bars—those rows of color patches you see on your prepress and press proofs—give proofing and press operators a way to control each step in the production process. Although most color bar elements require sophisticated equipment and training to analyze properly, an understanding of their uses can help you monitor the quality of your print project.

Prepress and print vendors purchase original film or the rights to digital files of color bars and other test images for each job. Because these images do not change from one print job to another, they serve as constant reference points throughout the proofing, platemaking, and press stages.

Color bars are essential troubleshooting tools at the proofing stage because they allow the vendor to evaluate the proof and determine the source of any variance from the expected image quality. They are also easy to analyze, both visually and with a *densitometer*—an instrument for measuring the relative density of any part of an image.

Digital files or original film of most color bars are supplied by numerous organizations, including E. I. Du Pont de Nemours (Du Pont), the Graphic Arts Technical Foundation (GATF), and the Rochester Institute of Technology.

Recognizing Color Bar Elements

Essentially, color bars and other test images are made up of small graphics (called *patches* or *elements*) of varying shapes, colors, tints, and patterns that are often grouped in rows. Each of the hundreds of elements currently in use by commercial prepress and press houses is designed for a specific purpose. Common color bar elements can be categorized as follows.

Solid-color patch. The most basic element of a test image is the solid-color patch—one for each of the process colors (cyan, magenta, yellow, and black). Solid-color patches are used to measure ink densities, according to industry or the print vendor's standards. Its geometric shape is usually a square and can be measured roughly by sight and precisely with a densitometer.

Tint patch. A tint patch is a solid-color patch whose color is less than 100%. Most color bars include several patches for each process color set at different tint percentages; the de facto standards in the United States are 25%, 50%, and 75% tints. Tint patches permit the measurement of dot gain because they are created by halftone screens (see "Compensating for Dot Gain on Press," page 78). Studies have shown that tint patches correlate more closely with the appearance of a color reproduction than solid patches because fluctuations in dot gain have more impact than solid ink density on color reproduction.

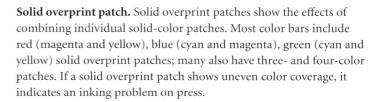

Solid overprint patch. Solid overprint patches show the effects of combining individual solid-color patches. Most color bars include red (magenta and yellow), blue (cyan and magenta), green (cyan and yellow) solid overprint patches; many also have three- and four-color patches. If a solid overprint patch shows uneven color coverage, it indicates an inking problem on press.

Tint overprint patch. Tint overprint patches combine tint patches of more than one color. *Gray-balance* tint overprint patches are particularly useful because these neutrals are made up of nearly equal amounts of cyan, magenta, and yellow (there is slightly more cyan than magenta and yellow). An imbalance in any one of these process colors—whether from incorrect ink density or from dot gain—can result in an easily detectable color cast in the patch.

Mechanical elements. A variety of color bar elements monitor mechanical deficiencies in the reproduction process. Elements such as the GATF Star Target (below left) are particularly sensitive to directional characteristics such as *slurring* (when round dots become football-shaped dots) or halftone-dot doubling.

Microline resolution targets of different shapes check problems that can affect resolution on film, proofs, and plates. The example of a microline resolution target shown on the right consists of 11-micron lines displayed in two directions and in negative (top half) and positive (bottom half) forms. If the proofing or platemaking settings are off, the positive 11-micron lines will fade away or the negative lines will fill with ink.

GATF Star Target   *Microline resolution target (magnified)*

Analyzing Test Images

You can measure color bars and other test images either visually or with an instrument. Elements that are designed for densitometric measurement can also be compared visually. Visual comparisons of color bars provide a subjective reference point for the accuracy of a production step; however, densitometers and other instruments are the only way to objectively control the production process.

Instrumental analysis. Prepress and press operators use two types of measurement systems to monitor production: *densitometry* (the measurement of reflectances) and *colorimetry* (the measurement of color). Densitometers are used in the former; colorimeters and spectrophotometers in the latter. Both the densitometer and the colorimeter use filters to take their measurements, while the more sensitive and expensive spectrophotometer does not. All three rely on mathematical equations to interpret color or reflectance in numerical form.

Tint and solid-color patches are two of the many test images designed for instrumental measurement. Although it is possible to see differences among them when they are viewed together, you can't know the degree of difference without taking a numerical measurement.

Visual analysis. Some elements, such as the GATF dot-gain scale, are specifically designed for visual analysis. With no dot gain, the numbers in the dot-gain scale remain nearly invisible (top version); with dot gain, the scale's numbers become dark and clearly visible (bottom version).

GATF dot-gain scale without (top) and with (bottom) dot gain on press

The GATF dot-gain scale is usually accompanied by a GATF slur gauge (an enlargement is shown here), which works in a similar manner. Without slur, the gauge remains nearly invisible; with slur, the word *slur* becomes visible to the naked eye.

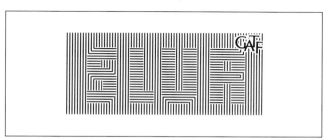

GATF slur gauge (enlarged)

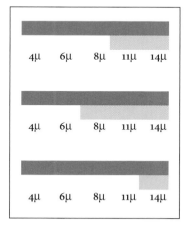

Another mechanical element designed for visual assessment is the microline exposure scale. The example shown here (created using tints rather than tiny microlines so you can see them better) shows the effects of three exposures on a positive Du Pont Cromalin™ proof. Since the proof is a positive, only the bottom microline blocks are relevant. When the exposure is set to Du Pont's recommended specifications, the proof "holds" the 11-microline patch while dropping the finer microlines (top). An underexposed proof holds microlines finer than 11 (middle), while an overexposed proof drops the 11-microline patch (bottom).

To speed printing time, print a low-resolution version of your file to a color digital proofing device. To do so, save the CMYK image in EPS format. In the EPS Format dialog box, select On (72 pixel/inch color) from the DCS pop-up menu.

Appendix: Utilizing PostScript

Understanding PostScript Error Messages

Customizing a PPD File

Utilizing PostScript

The PostScript language is the standard page description language for digital production whose workings are normally transparent to the user—until a PostScript error has occurred, that is.

A little knowledge of the PostScript language can greatly increase your productivity, however. This appendix presents two of many applications of the PostScript language: using PostScript error messages to guide you in working more efficiently and customizing PostScript printer privers for your production environment.

Understanding PostScript Error Messages

If a PostScript file fails to print because of an error, the experience can be frustrating, time-consuming, and, ultimately, expensive. Because the printing systems that support the PostScript language are complex, their error messages can be varied and difficult to diagnose. With some knowledge of the PostScript language and the environment in which it operates, though, these experiences can be reduced or even eliminated. This appendix provides a basis for understanding PostScript errors and ways to interpret and correct them.

What Is a PostScript Error?

When you print a page on a desktop printer or a RIP (see "What Is a RIP?" page 101) that supports the PostScript language, the printer or RIP executes an electronic file that is a representation of the page in PostScript code. More accurately, the printer or RIP contains software called the PostScript interpreter, which is responsible for executing the PostScript file and creating a second representation of the page (often called the raster image) that can be understood by a printer engine. The engine then prints the raster image on paper or film.

When the interpreter executes a PostScript file, the usual result is that the corresponding page or pages are printed by the printer engine. If there is something wrong with the PostScript code in this file, however, the interpreter will detect an error—a PostScript error. When such an error occurs, the interpreter executes special code, called an error handler, designed to address that particular error. The error handler records information in the RIP's memory about the error and then executes a command to stop processing the file.

At this point, the PostScript code in the file may ignore the command to stop processing so that the interpreter may continue executing the file. For example, a file's request for duplex (two-sided) printing on paper will likely cause an error if it's sent to a printer that prints on only one side of the paper. If so, the internal error handler for that error executes the command to stop the job. But the PostScript file may ignore the command to stop as well as the request for duplex printing (the source of the error). Although the job will not fail in this case, it will print only single-sided pages. If the PostScript code does not ignore the command to stop, the interpreter processes the information recorded earlier by the internal error handler, which usually produces a message that looks like this:

```
%%[ Error: <error name>; OffendingCommand: <command name> ]%%
%%[ Flushing: rest of job (to end-of-file) will be ignored ]%%
```

The first line shows the name of the error as well as the name of the PostScript command that caused the error. The second line states that the rest of the job will not be processed. (This particular error message is very useful, although you may not always be able to see it. See "Displaying Error Messages," page 102, for information on how to find error messages.) The interpreter will then stop executing the file.

The RIP may create other error messages that look like the one shown above. If the messages have a similar format but do not contain the words `Error` and `OffendingCommand`, however, they are very likely not PostScript errors. For example, you may see a message containing the label `PrinterError`, such as:

```
%%[ PrinterError: Media jam ]%%
```

This type of message does not represent an error in the PostScript file detected by the interpreter. It represents a different type of problem that was detected by some other part of the system, in this case by the printer engine.

Understanding Error Messages

Although you need to take some action to correct a PostScript error, you may not understand what the error is when you see the message corresponding to that error.

```
%%[ Error: limitcheck; OffendingCommand: sethalftone ]%%
```

If you see this message, for instance, you know that an error called `limitcheck` occurred when a command called `sethalftone` was executed in the file, but this message doesn't tell you much about the source of the problem. In some cases, you may get a clue from the name of the error or command involved. In this example, you might guess that the error was produced by some limit that was reached while attempting to set up a halftone screen.

You can make more educated guesses by learning about the types of commands and errors contained in the PostScript language. The *PostScript Language Reference Manual* (second edition) is the official specification for the PostScript language. It contains descriptions of all of the standard commands and errors contained in Level 2 of the PostScript language. The standard commands are commonly referred to as *operators*. Section 8.1, "Operator Summary," groups all of the operators in the PostScript language into twenty-four categories. It also contains a brief summary of the thirty possible PostScript errors.

When analyzing an error message, look first at the offending command to determine what type of operation failed. Then look at the name of the error to determine what kind of failure occurred. In both steps, use Section 8.1 as a guide. The error name alone is meaningless without also knowing the offending command. For example, a `limitcheck` error message means that some limit in the RIP's design was exceeded; by itself, however, a `limitcheck` error message tells you nothing about which limit or even what kind of limit was exceeded.

The offending command. The `OffendingCommand` statement identifies which PostScript operator failed. Operators may be divided into two groups: those that influence the appearance of a page and those that do not. In particular, operators in the first group influence the appearance of the three types of objects supported in the PostScript language: text, graphics, and images (images include rasterized artwork that has been generated digitally or scanned to capture pixel data). The distinction between the two groups is important: You may be able to correct errors resulting from operators in the first group by modifying the document from within the application that you used to create it. Operators in the second group, however, are used for the programming aspects of a PostScript file and require a great deal of experience with the PostScript language to understand and troubleshoot.

The first group of operators can be broken down further using the categories in Section 8.1 of the *PostScript Language Reference Manual,* which are described in Table 1: Graphics State, Device-Independent; Graphics State, Device-Dependent; Path Construction; Painting; Form and Pattern; Device Setup; and Character and Font. The large number of operators represented by these seven categories may be overwhelming, but bear in mind that within each category, some operators are seldom used. For example, the Painting operator `fill` occurs often because it is used to paint graphics; however, the Painting operator `ueofill` is rarely used because it is more specialized.

When you see an operator name in an error message's `OffendingCommand` statement, find its category in Section 8.1. This will help you identify the type of operation that produced the error. For example, the `show` operator is in the Character and Font category; therefore, if you see an error whose offending command is the `show` operator, you should suspect that there is a problem with the text in the PostScript file. Table 1 (page 102) lists the seven operator categories, along with their descriptions and common examples.

You may see some commands in error messages that you will not find in the *PostScript Language Reference Manual* because they are not standard PostScript commands. This situation is much more common in products that support only Level 1 of the PostScript language than in those that support Level 2 as well (see "PostScript Level 2," page 104).

The error name. After identifying the offending command in the error message, note the error name that was also reported in the message. The more common errors and their meanings are listed in Table 2 (pages 104-105), along with examples of offending commands and common problems and solutions for those combinations of errors and offending commands. Some of the examples are more complicated programming errors that require advanced debugging techniques and knowledge of the PostScript language to evaluate and correct. In such a case, you should call a local expert, the application vendor, or your RIP vendor for assistance.

You will find that the solutions offered in Table 2 do not always apply to the errors that you experience. There are too many possible errors— offending command combinations, circumstances that produce errors —and possible solutions to list in a single table. Instead, this information is intended to give you an idea of the usual meanings of common errors and how they vary.

To learn more about operators and errors, see Section 8.2, "Operator Details," of the *PostScript Language Reference Manual;* the rest of the manual describes the principles of operation regarding PostScript operators and errors. There are also a number of books and classes that discuss the PostScript language in more practical terms (see "Suggested Reading" and "Training Courses and Seminars," page 108).

What Is a RIP?

A raster image is a grid of pixels (picture elements) that represent the smallest sections of the page. Correspondingly, a *raster image processor* (RIP) is a system that contains the PostScript interpreter as well as additional hardware and software that send the raster image to a printer engine. The term RIP is used throughout this appendix to represent the device that receives and executes PostScript language files.

Displaying Error Messages

After the interpreter creates an error message, several things can happen to it, depending on the printer or RIP you are using. The message, perhaps in a different format than described earlier, may be recorded somewhere in the RIP, or it could be sent back to the computer that sent the file to the RIP.

If your RIP does not record messages or is unable to send them to an attached computer, the messages will be lost. In this case, it is best to use an error handler utility. Error handler utilities are PostScript files that change the way error messages are processed and displayed by the interpreter. For example, they may print the error information at the RIP or write it to the RIP's disk so that it may be read later. Some error handler utilities also provide more information than just the error message, but this additional information typically requires in-depth knowledge of the PostScript language. Contact your RIP vendor for information on available error handler utilities. Adobe Systems also provides a simple error handler utility via modem or the Internet (see "Accessing Adobe Files," page *103*).

Even if the RIP can send error messages back to your computer, you may not see the error message at all or it may flash by too quickly on your computer's display to be read or understood. In this case, the printer driver on your computer is ignoring or intercepting messages sent back from a RIP. (Examples of printer drivers include Apple Computer's LaserWriter driver, Microsoft's PSCRIPT™ driver, and Adobe Systems' PSPrinter™ and ADOBEPS™ drivers for the Macintosh and Windows platforms, respectively.)

TABLE 1: POSTSCRIPT OPERATORS			
OPERATOR CATEGORY	**CATEGORY DESCRIPTION**	**SAMPLE OPERATORS**	**OPERATOR DESCRIPTIONS**
Graphics State, Device-Independent	Used to control how objects are painted; results should not vary from one type of output-device engine to another	setcolor setlinewidth	Establishes the color for an object to be painted Establishes the thickness of painted lines
Graphics State, Device-Dependent	Used to control how objects are painted; results usually vary from one type of output-device engine to another	sethalftone setflat	Establishes a requested halftone screen Establishes the flatness of curves
Path Construction	Used to create graphics such as polygons and curves	lineto curveto arc	Draws a line Draws a curve Draws part or all of a circle
Painting	Used to paint graphics and images	stroke fill image	Paints the outline of graphics Paints the interior of graphics Paints images
Form and Pattern	Used to generate repeatable forms and patterns	setpattern execform	Establishes a pattern Paints a form
Device Setup	Used to set up printing attributes	setpagedevice	Installs requested device features
Character and Font	Used to manipulate fonts and parts of fonts, such as characters	findfont show	Looks for and loads a requested font Paints a character or group of characters

You can get an error handler utility and other files from Adobe Systems through the following on-line sources:

- **CompuServe:** Type `go adobe`.

- **Adobe BBS:** Set your modem to 8 data bits, 1 stop bit, no parity, and up to 14.4 KBs. Using a terminal emulation program that supports VT-100 or ANSI emulation, dial 408-562-6839, and type in your name and a password. You can find and download the files required to communicate with the BBS by selecting New User Info, then FC Client Interface.

- **Anonymous FTP:** Connect to `ftp.adobe.com (130.248.1.4)`; enter `anonymous` as the user name and your e-mail address as the password. The Adobe Developer's Association General Information is in the file `long.help` in the directory `/pub/adobe/Documents`. An error handler utility is in the file `ehandler.ps` in the directory `/pub/adobe/Programs`.

- **Electronic mail:** Send a message to the Internet address `ps-file-server@adobe.com` with the word `help` in the subject line. The server will send instructions back to you in a mail message. You can get a copy of the `ehandler.ps` file by typing `send programs ehandler.ps` in the body of the e-mail message you send to the e-mail server.

Note that Adobe does not provide direct end-user technical support for the PostScript language. There is a forum for such questions on the Internet called `comp.lang.postscript`.

Further, if the printer driver detects that the message represents an error, it may post an uninformative message such as `-8133`, which indicates that a PostScript error has occurred. Be aware that not all generic error messages indicate a PostScript error. For example, the messages `-4100` or `The job is OK but can't be printed.` on the Macintosh may indicate a problem in the communications link between the Macintosh and the RIP.

You can use an error handler utility in this case, but this is not always the best choice. An error handler utility that instructs the RIP to print the error information on paper or film, for instance, could be an expensive waste of media. A better method is to look for an option to display error messages when you print. The PSPrinter and LaserWriter 8.0 printer drivers (from Adobe Systems and Apple Computer, respectively) both provide this option.

If this feature is not available to you, the next best method is to save the PostScript file on your computer's hard disk drive and download it separately to the RIP. Look for an option to save the PostScript file when you print. After saving the file, send it to the RIP using a downloader utility. (Examples of downloader utilities are font downloader software, LaserTalk™, and SendPS™, all of which are available from Adobe Systems; your RIP vendor may also offer downloader utilities.)

Typically, downloader utilities either show you the error message on-screen after sending the file or write any information returned by the RIP to a "log file" on your computer's hard disk drive. Alternatively, if your error handler utility provides additional information from the RIP with the error message and does not print on media, install it and then download the saved PostScript file. This allows you to see the more complete information returned by the error handler utility.

Follow these steps to help you determine which method to use to display complete error messages:

1. If the RIP can record or display error messages, consult the RIP documentation on how to read them. If not, go to step 2.

2. If the RIP is unable to send messages back to your computer, use an error handler utility. If it can send messages back, go to step 3.

3. If you are able to see complete error messages when you print, begin using them. If not, go to step 4.

4. If your printer driver has an option to display complete error messages, enable this option when you print. If not, go to step 5.

5. If your printer driver has an option to save PostScript files, save the file, then use a downloader utility to send the file to the RIP.

6. Finally, try running the PostScript file through the Adobe Acrobat Distiller. If the Distiller detects the same error, you should be able to see what that error is.

If none of these methods works, you will need to use more advanced techniques. Consult with a local expert or contact your RIP vendor for assistance.

Printer Drivers

Software programs that convert an application's representation of a document into equivalent PostScript code are called printer drivers. In simple terms, printer drivers tell the printer what to do. Some applications, such as Adobe Illustrator, Adobe Photoshop, and QuarkXPress®, create their own PostScript code for the documents they print. This code allows an application to control the appearance of a document. The resulting code may be further modified by the printer driver – for example, to request that certain features be used by the RIP. Software applications that do not create PostScript code use printer drivers to do so.

PostScript Level 2

Adobe Systems introduced PostScript Level 2 in 1990. It includes all of the operators found in Level 1 systems, as well as several new operators. For example, Level 2 includes a single operator, setpagedevice, for requesting printing features from a product. In Level 1, by contrast, each product had its own set of device-dependent commands for making such requests. Also, Level 2 uses memory more effectively than Level 1 does. Fewer memory-related errors occur in PostScript Level 2 products.

TABLE 2: POSTSCRIPT ERROR MESSAGES			
ERROR NAME	USUAL MEANING	OFFENDING COMMANDS	COMMON PROBLEMS AND SOLUTIONS
<fontname> not found, using Courier.	The requested font was not supplied by the RIP or was not within the PostScript file. (This error message is formatted differently; it has no offending command.)	Not applicable	Download the missing font to the RIP, include it in the document, or choose a different font.
configurationerror	A requested feature setting cannot be satisfied; often accompanied by an extra ErrorInfo field in the error message indicating the requested feature.	setpagedevice	Do not request the feature from the printer driver, use a different printer support file, or configure the RIP to support the feature.
dictfull	There is no more room in PostScript data structures called dictionaries; this problem is more common with PostScript Level 1 than with Level 2.	store, put, def	These operators store objects in dictionaries; error requires advanced debugging.
invalidaccess	An attempt was made to put an object into a read-only data structure.	store, put, def	These operators store objects in various PostScript data structures; error requires advanced debugging.
invalidfont	There was an attempt to install a malformed or an improperly licensed font in the RIP's memory.	findfont, definefont, selectfont	Replace or reinstall the font on the RIP and/or computer.
invalidrestore	There is a programming problem with memory management.	restore	There is likely a problem with the printer driver; requires advanced debugging.
ioerror	An input/output error occurred while the RIP was processing a file; the file in question could be the actual job or another file referenced by the job file.	image, colorimage	The amount of data supplied is incorrect; scan, edit, or import the image again.
		Random characters	These characters may indicate a problem with the communications link; move or replace the communications line, check communications settings, disable spoolers, or run the job again.
limitcheck	An implementation limit was exceeded.	show, fill, stroke, clip, other painting operators	A graphic is too complex (this occurs very rarely when using PostScript Level 2); increase flatness, split paths, simplify the graphic, or lower the printer engine's resolution.
		sethalftone	The internal representation of the requested halftone screen is too large or too small; consult your RIP vendor.
		image	The image is too large, its resolution is too high, or it cannot be rotated. Reduce the size or resolution, rotate the image at a different angle, or rotate it in an image editing application such as Adobe Photoshop.

TABLE 2: POSTSCRIPT ERROR MESSAGES (CONTINUED)			
ERROR NAME	**USUAL MEANING**	**OFFENDING COMMANDS**	**COMMON PROBLEMS AND SOLUTIONS**
rangecheck	A value provided to the operator was outside the acceptable range.	setpapertray (Level 1)	The requested paper tray does not exist; request a different tray from the printer driver.
		Several operators	Requires advanced debugging
stackoverflow	This is a programming problem concerning the filling up of an internal data structure called the operand stack.	Several operators	May indicate a printer driver problem or interference from a separate utility; requires advanced debugging.
stackunderflow	The operator expected one or more values to be available on the operand stack, but there were none.	Several operators	May indicate a printer driver problem or interference from a separate utility; requires advanced debugging.
timeout	A time limit for an operation has been exceeded.	Several operators	A time-out threshold is set too low or there is a communications problem. Use administration software or the printer driver to reset the time-out value on the RIP, or try a different driver.
typecheck	The operator expected a certain type of value on the operand stack, but the wrong type was provided instead.	Several operators	May be a printer driver problem or interference from a separate utility; requires advanced debugging.
		Random or no characters	This could indicate a problem with the communications link or with the leftover data in the job; try a different communications line or printer driver. This problem may also occur if a PostScript file is saved, transferred to a different computer platform, and downloaded from that computer; try saving the file in ASCII or Text Only rather than binary format.
undefined	The name specified in the OffendingCommand is not known to the RIP.	md	This is not a PostScript operator; it indicates that the required PostScript code has not been included in a PostScript file saved on the Macintosh. Resave the file.
		Several operators	The job contains a nonstandard operator that is not recognized by the RIP; check the driver settings or select a different printer support file.
		Random characters	Too much data for an image may have been supplied; scan, edit, or import the image again.
VMerror	The RIP has run out of PostScript virtual memory (VM) during the job.	Several operators	Reboot the RIP to clear its memory; this error should be very rare when using PostScript Level 2.

When a driver inserts PostScript code that requests a certain feature of the RIP, the file becomes specific to that RIP. This is commonly referred to as a *device-dependent file*. Without this kind of feature code, the file is a pure page description and is considered a *device-independent file*. Sending a device-dependent file to the wrong RIP can cause PostScript errors.

Causes of PostScript Errors

In order to correct a PostScript error, you first need to know at which point in the printing process it was introduced. Although printing a document is a complex operation that varies slightly from one printing environment to another, generally there is a common sequence of steps. If you become familiar with these steps, you will be better able to isolate the cause of the errors you encounter. The following list describes each step in the printing process, along with common problems associated with it and suggested solutions.

1. You compose a document on your computer using an application. The application uses its own graphics language to represent the document on your monitor. The document may also include files imported from other applications. If there is a problematic object in this document or an error in one of the imported files, remove or modify the offending object or imported file.

2. When you print the document, you select the destination RIP as well as various settings for printing the document on that RIP, such as paper size, hardware resolution, or flatness. If you selected settings that are inappropriate for the RIP, try selecting different ones.

3. The printer driver then converts the document into a PostScript file. The driver translates the representation of the document from the application's graphics language into the PostScript language. If the PostScript code created by the printer driver is faulty, the translation will produce an error. Try a different printer driver or try modifying the document from within the application.

4. Some printer drivers add information to the PostScript code, such as details about fonts, images, and other resources required by a document. Such information can be formatted according to the Document Structuring Conventions (DSC) described in the *PostScript Language Reference Manual* or the Open Prepress Interface (OPI) specification. If there is a mistake in the added information, a problem in the PostScript code may be introduced later if a spooler is attached to the RIP. Try using a different driver, changing the fonts, or changing the structure of the document (by moving or deleting pages, for example).

5. The printer driver may insert extra PostScript code into the file (see "Sending the Right File," this page) that requests specific features of the destination RIP. Some printer drivers obtain this code from printer support files, such as PostScript Printer Description (PPD) files from Adobe Systems (see "Customizing a PPD File," page 108). These support files contain product-specific code so that the printer drivers

don't have to include it. If you or the printer driver chooses the wrong printer support file for the destination RIP, go back and select the appropriate printer support file for the RIP. If the information in the printer support file is incorrect, contact your RIP vendor or try using a printer support file for a very similar RIP.

6. The PostScript file is sent or transferred to the RIP, usually by the printer driver. If there is a problem with the way that the file is sent to the RIP, either in the physical connection or in the software that is sending the file, try a different way of sending the file. For example, try a different cable, using a different type of communications link, or using the same link but a different printer driver, downloader, or file transfer software.

7. If a spooler or OPI server is on the network or part of the RIP, the spooler or server intercepts the file. (A spooler is software that coordinates the delivery of files to a RIP.) Some spoolers and servers modify the file according to the DSC or OPI information in the file before passing it on to the PostScript interpreter within the RIP. If the DSC or OPI information is incorrect or if the spooler handles the information incorrectly, an error will result. Disable the spooler if possible, or check that the resources required by the file are available at the RIP.

8. Finally, the interpreter executes the file—this is when errors are actually detected. Problems within the interpreter itself are less common than errors introduced in the previous steps. Some utilities, such as those for color calibration, make subtle changes to the interpreter's operation that can interfere with the proper operation of the interpreter. If there is a problem in the interpreter or if a utility is interfering, try either using a different RIP or restarting the RIP without using specialized utilities. If this does not help, contact your RIP vendor to report the problem.

If all else fails, one final solution that you can try is to save the PostScript file, modify it directly, and download it to the RIP. This requires explicit knowledge of the PostScript language and of DSC, however. Alternatively, you can contact your RIP vendor for assistance.

Isolating the Cause of the Error

Note that one common action in the suggested solutions is to replace, remove, or otherwise change a particular part in the process, such as the printer driver, printer support file, or spooler. The best way to find the cause of an error is to isolate it by systematically changing one part of the process at a time and then observing whether the error still occurs. If you make a change and the problem disappears, you have located the cause of the problem and solved it as well; otherwise, try changing another part of the process.

Replacing the printer driver is a common change, since the driver is involved in several of the steps in the printing process. If you try a different driver, you are sending different PostScript code for the same document. (Some applications, such as Adobe Photoshop, Adobe Illustrator, and QuarkXPress, generate their own PostScript code, so changing the driver may not have an effect in these cases.) If the error persists, then you need to look at the other parts of the process, such as modifying the file from within the application or changing the way the file is transferred to the RIP.

If you modify the file in the application, you can use a similarly systematic approach by replacing, removing, or modifying pages or objects on the page. Again, the error information may guide you in determining which objects to change.

There are several ways to change the method for transferring a file to the RIP. You can try different physical connections, such as LocalTalk® or EtherTalk® (both from Apple Computer) or serial or parallel cables. Or you can save a PostScript file using the printer driver and then send it to the RIP separately with a downloader utility. In this case, you are using the downloader utility software to transfer the file to the RIP; if the error disappears, you know it had to do with the way the printer driver transferred the file.

When you save a PostScript file using a printer driver, however, you may introduce some new problems. Because the driver adds device-dependent code to the file, it may not be appropriate to send the file to another type of RIP; either the file will fail or you will not get the printing features you requested. Also, if you transfer a saved PostScript file from a Windows or DOS machine to a Macintosh, there may be nonprinting characters (also called binary characters) within the file that will cause an undefined error when the file is downloaded to the RIP. In general, files with binary characters are much more difficult to transfer from one computer platform to another. It's safest to save files in ASCII text format rather than binary format.

Another method for transferring the PostScript file is to store the file on the RIP's internal disk, if it has one, and run it from there. This is similar to downloading and storing a font to the RIP's internal disk. When you run the file from the RIP's disk, you no longer need to send the file to print it, which effectively removes the communications step from the printing process. (Note, however, that if the file had binary

characters in it when you stored it on the RIP's disk, those characters may have been lost if you used a serial or parallel connection.)

Some downloader utilities allow you to store a PostScript file to the RIP's internal disk. If one is not available, use a text editor (in ASCII format) to add the following PostScript code to the beginning of a PostScript file:

```
%!
/rf currentfile def
/wf (myfile.ps) (w) file def
/str 65535 string def

  //rf //str readstring
  //wf 3 -1 roll writestring
  not {exit} if
} bind loop
```

You can change the name of the file by replacing *myfile.ps* in the code with your file name (retain the parentheses). It's best to keep the name simple and to avoid using spaces or nonalphanumeric characters. You can then send this new file to the RIP using a downloader utility. If there are no problems, the PostScript file will now be stored on the RIP's internal disk. Next, from within the text editor, create another PostScript file that contains only this simple code:

```
%!
(myfile.ps) run
```

Again, substitute the placeholder *myfile.ps* with the name of the file you stored previously on the RIP's internal disk. Save (also in ASCII format) and download this simple file to the RIP. The file *myfile.ps* will be executed. You can send this file as many times as you want to run *myfile.ps*. If the error persists, then the source of the problem is not in the communications line or the way that the printer driver sent the file to the RIP. Once you have finished testing for the error's source, you must delete the *myfile.ps* file; to do so, create and download another PostScript file to the RIP that contains this code:

```
%!
(myfile.ps) deletefile
```

Your RIP vendor may have utilities or methods available for performing these kinds of operations with PostScript files. For example, on some software-based RIPs that run on workstations, it may be possible

Changing the Printing Process

The easiest way to vary a part of the printing process – such as the driver, printer support file, or spooler – is to replace that part. If possible, try to remove it from the process. For example, disabling a spooler simplifies file transfer, while rebooting a RIP without downloading utility software simplifies the operation of the interpreter.

Getting Started

Following are some general guidelines to use when you are customizing a PPD file:

- Make one change at a time to reduce the complexity of any error debugging that might be required later.

- Test each change thoroughly before using the PPD file in a production environment.

- Before attempting extensive changes, become familiar with the latest PPD file specifications (see "Accessing Adobe Files," page 103, for on-line sources for this file).

- Always document changes you make to a PPD file and when you made them.

to store a PostScript file on the workstation's file system so that it can be executed by the RIP.

This systematic approach can be time-consuming, since the printing process has so many parts and steps. Bear in mind, however, that the PostScript error message will often provide clues about the type of operation that failed and how it failed. For example, if you see an ioerror message with random characters rather than an operator name as the offending command, you should suspect a problem with the communications link to the RIP. But if you see an ioerror message associated with the image operator (related to a scanned image), you should either suspect the communications link or the application that you used to create and save the scanned image.

With time and experience, you will discover that intuitive hunches play a part in determining the causes of PostScript errors. Yet even when you are able to make such intuitive leaps, it will always be a good idea to return to basic principles: Know the steps in the printing process, know how to display the complete error message, know how to interpret the elements of the error message, and know that successful troubleshooting requires systematically isolating possible sources of the problem.

Suggested Reading

Braswell, Frank. *Inside PostScript.* Berkeley, Calif.: Peachpit Press, 1989.

Fink, Peter. *PostScript Screening: Adobe Accurate Screens.* Mountain View, Calif.: Adobe Press/MacMillan Computer Publishing, 1992.

Glover, Gary. *Running PostScript from MS-DOS.* Blue Ridge, Pa.: Windcrest Books, 1989.

McGilton, Henry, and Mary Campione. *PostScript by Example.* Reading, Mass.: Addison-Wesley, 1992.

Adobe Systems Incorporated. *PostScript Language Reference Manual.* 2d ed. Reading, Mass.: Addison-Wesley, 1990.

Reid, Glenn. *Thinking in PostScript.* Reading, Mass.: Addison-Wesley, 1990.

Roth, Stephen. *Real World PostScript.* Reading, Mass.: Addison-Wesley, 1988.

Smith, Ross. *Learning PostScript: A Visual Approach.* Berkeley, Calif.: Peachpit Press, 1990.

Training Courses and Seminars

PostScript Language Training, Levels 1 and 2
Acquired Knowledge
619-587-4668

PostScript Concepts Seminar
Systems of Merritt
205-660-1240

Customizing a PPD File

A PostScript Printer Description (PPD) file—a printer support file in ASCII text format created by Adobe Systems or one of its original equipment manufacturers (OEMs)—describes the specifications and features of a specific PostScript printing device in its original manufactured state. Applications such as Adobe Separator and PageMaker, as well as printer drivers from Adobe Systems and Apple Computer, use PPD files, which may be distributed by the application vendor or OEM. PPD files allow the user to select settings for different features, such as paper sizes, tray options, halftone screens, and output resolutions. Sometimes you may need to add to or modify a PPD file for a particular printing environment. This section—which is addressed primarily to prepress operators—discusses common ways of customizing PPD files.

In general, modifying a PPD file requires knowledge of the PPD format and often of the PostScript language itself. Although neither Adobe Systems nor its OEMs support PPD file customization, with careful attention to detail, it can be done successfully.

Customization Methods

Changes can be made to a PPD file in two ways: by editing the PPD file directly with a text editor, or by creating and editing a separate PPD file, called an editable customization file, that refers to the original PPD file. If you edit the PPD file, save a copy of the original and edit the copy, not the original. Use any text editor to modify or create the PPD file and always save the file in Text Only or ASCII format.

To create an editable customization file, create a new file in a text editor and type the following line:

```
*Include: "filename"
```

Replace *filename* (keep the quotes) with the name of the original PPD file that is to be customized. Add the custom PPD entries you want before this line so it will override the information in the original PPD file. The custom PPD entries must conform to the PPD specifications. Save the customization file with a unique name that represents the changes you made or the particular device for which you made those changes (for example, `MyPrntr.PPD`). The `.PPD` extension (it is not case-sensitive) should be preserved because many applications and print managers search for files with that extension. Store both the original PPD file and the customization file in the same location.

Whenever possible, use the editable customization file method rather than editing a PPD file directly. There are several advantages to using an editable customization file over modifying the PPD file. First, the editable customization file method allows you to isolate errors more easily. Second, the original PPD files are still supported by Adobe Systems and its OEMs because they remain unchanged. Third, you can create a naming convention for the editable customization files that will make it easy to track future modifications. The disadvantage of using an editable customization file is that you must know the PPD file specifications in order to make the correct entries.

The only time you should edit the original PPD file is when you wish to make a small number of simple changes. In general, if you are making several customizations, you should use the editable customization file method instead.

Applications

This section provides some examples of PPD file customizations.

Editing halftone screen information. The `ColorSepScreenAngle` and `ColorSepScreenFreq` entries in either an original PPD or a customization file correspond to a particular halftone screen angle and frequency for each process and custom color, usually at a certain output resolution. Although you may select a 132-lpi screen frequency and a 2540-dpi output resolution in the dialog boxes of an application such as Adobe Separator, the actual settings may not represent an exact 132-lpi screen. To set your own custom screen frequency and angle, follow these steps.

1. Search for the `ColorSepScreenAngle` and `ColorSepScreenFreq` entries in the PPD file (they are usually near the end).

2. Locate the group of lines representing the screen frequency and output resolution combination (in lpi and dpi, respectively) you wish to modify (132/2540 in this example). You will find lines of code similar to these:

```
*% For 132 lpi / 2540 dpi

*ColorSepScreenAngle ProcessBlack.132lpi.2540dpi/132 lpi / 2540 dpi: "45.0"

*ColorSepScreenAngle CustomColor.132lpi.2540dpi/132 lpi / 2540 dpi: "45.0"

*ColorSepScreenAngle ProcessCyan.132lpi.2540dpi/132 lpi / 2540 dpi: "18.4349"

*ColorSepScreenAngle ProcessMagenta.132lpi.2540dpi/132 lpi / 2540 dpi: "71.565"

*ColorSepScreenAngle ProcessYellow.132lpi.2540dpi/132 lpi / 2540 dpi: "0.0"

*ColorSepScreenFreq ProcessBlack.132lpi.2540dpi/132 lpi / 2540 dpi: "119.737"

*ColorSepScreenFreq CustomColor.132lpi.2540dpi/132 lpi / 2540 dpi: "119.737"

*ColorSepScreenFreq ProcessCyan.132lpi.2540dpi/132 lpi / 2540 dpi: "133.871"

*ColorSepScreenFreq ProcessMagenta.132lpi.2540dpi/132 lpi / 2540 dpi: "133.871"

*ColorSepScreenFreq ProcessYellow.132lpi.2540dpi/132 lpi / 2540 dpi: "127.0"
```

3. At the end of each `ColorSepScreenAngle` line, edit the value within the quotation marks. This will change the angle of the screen used to create the halftone. These numbers must contain a decimal point, so follow each whole number with a decimal point and a zero. For example, enter 45 degrees as `"45.0"` (include quotation marks). If you are using the customization file method, copy these entries and place them in the customization file before the line containing `*Include`. Then edit the values in the customization file.

4. At the end of each `ColorSepScreenFreq` line, edit the value within the quotation marks. This will change the screen frequency used to create the halftone. These numbers must also have a decimal point, so follow each whole number with a decimal point and a zero. For example, enter 127 degrees as `"127.0"` (include quotation marks).

Changing menu item names. Applications and drivers use translation strings to describe some menu items. Translation strings translate potentially cryptic PPD file entries into easily identifiable names or phrases, even in natural programming languages. To identify a translation string in a PPD file, look for a phrase preceded by a solidus (/) and followed by a colon (:). By editing these strings, you can use names that are more useful to you than the printer vendor's names.

For example, many imagesetter PPDs have a paper-size selection called Letter.Transverse, for letter-sized paper that is fed into the printer by its long edge. It may be more intuitive to be able to select the Long-edge-feed Letter paper size than it is to select the Letter.Transverse size

If you have trouble printing a multi-page document, try to pinpoint where the Postscript error is by printing the document one page at a time. When you find a page that will not print, try printing it without any graphic elements first. If the page prints without the graphic elements, try adding them one at a time until you isolate an element that could be the causing the Postscript error.

in the appropriate dialog box. You can customize the PPD file to change the name of this paper size.

The latest drivers from Adobe Systems and Apple Computer use the *PageSize entries in the PPD file to display the names of the available paper sizes in the appropriate dialog box. When the entry shown below exists, it causes the printer driver to display Letter.Transverse, since there is no translation string. (In a PPD file, these entries are placed with other *PageSize entries; in a customization file, they are placed above the line that contains *Include.)

PageSize Letter.Transverse: "<PostScript language code>*"

 Change the menu item by adding the following translation string :

PageSize Letter.Transverse/Long-edge-feed Letter: "<PostScript language code>*"

In this case, as a result of this new entry, the name of this paper size will now be displayed as Long-edge-feed Letter the next time you select the same PPD file. Do not change the PostScript language code between the quotes.

Changing the nickname of your printer. There may be times when you'll need to identify a PPD file by the function of the printer it represents, rather than the name of the product. The PSPrinter driver from Adobe Systems, for example, is able to display an alternate name for a PPD file when you select the printer in the Chooser on a Macintosh. Changing the *NickName entry in the PPD file changes this alternate name.

First, find the *NickName entry, which is usually near the beginning of the PPD file. It will look something like this:

*NickName: "ACME Color Printer 1000 v2013.114"

You may change the nickname to something more useful to you by changing the *NickName statement to read:

*NickName: "ACME Color Proofer"

The new nickname should be no longer than thirty-one characters. If it is longer, add this entry: ShortNickName: "*<desired name>*"

Contributors' Biographies

Patrick Ames is the editor in chief of Adobe Press at Adobe Systems. He has previously worked as a book publishing consultant, as a publications and production manager at Apple Computer, and as the publisher of Breitenbush Books. He is the author of *Beyond Paper* (Adobe Press, 1993) and conducts seminars and workshops on designing electronic documents, books, and magazines for on-screen usage.

Rita Amladi is a product support engineer for Adobe Technical Support at Adobe Systems, where she has helped develop several releases of Adobe Photoshop, Adobe Illustrator, and Adobe Streamline over the past five years. Ms. Amladi has made presentations at the National Press Photographers Association (NPPA) Electronic Workshops and the Palm Beach Photographic Workshops, and before other groups in the United States and Japan. Prior to joining Adobe, Ms. Amladi worked as a sales consultant with a computer reseller. She holds a bachelor of fine arts in graphic design from the University of San Francisco and a bachelor of fine arts in design from the Sir J. J. School of Architecture and Design in Bombay, India.

Sandy Bozek owns and operates Bozek Desktop, a desktop publishing consultancy specializing in project management, systems integration, and training for design, printing, and publishing environments. Ms. Bozek began her career as a journeyman offset stripper at French Bray Printing and later moved into sales. Since then, she has worked as a production manager for the Adams Group and as director of production for Credit Card Service. Ms. Bozek teaches at Montgomery College, at the Maryland Institute of Art, and at the Printing Industries of Maryland; she is also coauthor of *Photoshop in Black and White* (Peachpit Press, 1994).

E. M. Ginger is a writer and editor who has worked with type and typography for two decades. She was managing editor of the journal *Fine Print* for twelve years and the editor of several best-selling cookbooks. She is a typographic consultant and freelance writer in the San Francisco Bay Area.

Barry Haynes has returned to photography after spending ten years working on software development and research at Apple Computer. Mr. Haynes uses digital technology to print, show, and sell his photography; he is also a digital-imaging consultant. Mr. Haynes teaches courses in Adobe Photoshop for such clients as Nikon, Eastman Kodak, Apple Computer, Sony, Pacific Bell, Tandem, the *San Jose Mercury News,* and the *Sacramento Bee.* He conducts digital photography workshops for the Center for Creative Imaging, the Palm Beach Photographic Workshops, Seybold Seminars, the American Society of Magazine Photographers, and several advertising agencies and design firms. He is currently working on a combination book and CD-ROM about advanced Photoshop techniques.

Michael Heth owns Chesttop Publishing, a San Anselmo, California, screen-printing company that creates and prints high-definition images on textiles using proprietary techniques he developed with Adobe Photoshop. Mr. Heth has consulted for Adobe Systems, Fractal Design, and LightSource.

George Jardine was a professional photographer for over ten years before getting involved with computer applications in the graphic arts. His work has appeared in *Interior Design, Better Homes & Gardens,* and *Sports Illustrated* magazines, as well as *USA Today* and many other national publications. After spending several years in the electronic prepress field, Mr. Jardine now lives and works in Mountain View, California, and takes freelance assignments in photocomposition, 3-D animation, and multimedia production. He also leads seminars in the United States and Japan.

Lisa Jeans is a graphic designer for Adobe Systems, where she has worked for over four years. During her three years as a member of the Adobe Special Projects Group, she served as designer and author for *Design Essentials* (Adobe Press, 1992) and as designer for *Imaging Essentials* (Adobe Press, 1993). Ms. Jeans holds a bachelor of science degree in graphic design from California Polytechnic State University, San Luis Obispo.

Karl Kuntz is the managing editor of graphics for the *Columbus Dispatch,* with primary responsibility for the newspaper's visual content and its art, design, photography, and color departments. Mr. Kuntz began his newspaper career as a copy clerk and has since worked as a studio photographer, newspaper staff photographer, picture editor, graphics editor, Scitex operator, and assistant managing editor at several newspapers. Mr. Kuntz teaches newspaper layout and design at Ohio State University, writes a monthly column for *Newspapers and Technology* related to digital photography, and is a member of the National Press Photographers Association.

Mattias Nyman is an independent consultant who has specialized in electronic prepress and color reproduction since 1987. He is the author of *Four Colors/One Image* (Peachpit Press, 1993) and lives in Stockholm, Sweden.

Jim Rich is president of Rich & Associates, a consulting firm in the Washington, D.C., area that specializes in publishing, college-level curriculum development, research, and prepress-industry training programs. Mr. Rich has been affiliated with Adobe Systems, the Center for Creative Imaging, Crosfield Electronics, Electronics for Imaging, The Lanman Companies, the National Geographic Society, Miles/ Agfa, Montgomery College, and the Rochester Institute of Technology. He is the coauthor of *Photoshop in Black and White* (Peachpit Press, 1994) and has contributed to *Imaging Essentials* (Adobe Press, 1993), *Desktop Color Separation* (Graphic Arts Publishing, 1993), and several magazines, including *Pre, Mac PrePress,* and *Southern Graphics.* Mr. Rich holds a master's degree in printing technology from the Rochester Institute of Technology.

Grant Ruiz is a consulting engineer at Adobe Systems, where he provides technical assistance to companies developing products based on Adobe's Configurable PostScript Interpreter (CPSI). Since joining Adobe in 1990, Mr. Ruiz has worked primarily on troubleshooting high-resolution imagesetters. He has authored and contributed to papers and classes on such subjects as PostScript language programming, raster image processor (RIP) architecture, and digital halftoning. Previously, Mr. Ruiz worked for Xerox in the development of fonts and applications for document creation and printing. Mr. Ruiz holds a degree in mathematics from Pomona College.

Jim Ryan is a product support engineer for Adobe Systems' graphics products, specializing in Adobe Illustrator. In his four years with Adobe Systems, he has served as a customer support specialist in

Graphics Technical Support and as a production artist in Adobe Systems' Technical Publications department. Mr. Ryan has written several plug-in programs for Adobe Illustrator 5.5, including the Document Info plug-in.

Mark Samworth is a technical specialist with E. I. Du Pont de Nemours and currently works in digital-proof color matching. Prior to this assignment, he was involved in the technological development of desktop imaging; his work there received patents in the areas of tone reproduction, duotone imaging, and imagesetter calibration. He started his career with Du Pont as a color specialist in flexographic printing, concentrating on scanner setup for flexo, process control, and color proofing. He received his bachelor of science in printing technology from the Rochester Institute of Technology and his master of business administration from the University of Delaware.

Mark Siprut is a consultant and teacher specializing in computer graphics and desktop publishing. He is a lecturer in graphic design at San Diego State University and holds both an master of fine arts in printmaking and a master's degree in photography. Mr. Siprut has conducted workshops at the University of California at San Diego, the University of California at Santa Barbara, Humboldt State University, and Platt College. He has contributed articles on digital imaging to various publications and is the revision author of the *Adobe Photoshop Handbook* (Random House, 1994).

Pat Soberanis has been an editorial consultant in San Francisco since 1986. Specializing in computer technology and digital print and multimedia production, she writes, edits, and provides production services for book and magazine publishers and for corporations. Among her clients are Adobe Press; Macmillan Computer Publishing; *Publish, OnLine Design, Upside,* and *NewMedia* magazines; and Autodesk, Inc.

Diane Tapscott has over eighteen years of experience in publishing, print production, and marketing communications, specializing in the international marketplace. An independent writer, editor, and project-management consultant, she owns and operates Whirly Girl Press in Portola Valley, California. Ms. Tapscott has held positions at Atari, Apple Computer, and Adobe Systems managing design, production, and international marketing communications; she began her career writing how-to books for Sunset Books. A graduate of Syracuse University in fashion and fabric design, Ms. Tapscott is beginning a book project on decorative arts and printing using digital tools and applications.

Peter Truskier is technology manager at Star Graphic Arts, a full-service prepress company in Foster City, California. He has worked as an offset press operator, stripper, color-separation photographer, and scanner operator. Since 1985, he has been operating and managing electronic prepress systems. Mr. Truskier is a lead beta tester for such companies as Adobe Systems, Apple Computer, Next, Scenicsoft, Scitex, and others. He has written numerous portions of application and PostScript software to address specific production requirements. He attended the Massachusetts Institute of Technology and graduated from the University of California at Berkeley.

Bret Waters is president of Metagraphics, a PostScript color prepress and electronic art production company in Palo Alto, California. Metagraphics provided prepress services for *Imaging Essentials* (Adobe Press, 1993) and *Production Essentials* (Adobe Press, 1994) and also produces annual reports, packaging, books, and brochures for a number of computer software and hardware companies, advertising agencies, and graphic design firms. Before founding Metagraphics, Mr. Waters spent ten years in the commercial printing and conventional color prepress business.

Steve Werner is the training manager at Rapid in San Francisco, a full-service prepress company. He teaches graphic artists how to prepare artwork for prepress in Macintosh graphics applications. He has been a production manager in Macintosh-based digital prepress since 1986 and has taught on the subject since 1988. He is coauthor of the forthcoming book, *Guaranteed Color* (Random House, Spring 1995).

Bibliography

ADOBE SYSTEMS INCORPORATED. *PostScript Language Reference Manual.* 2d ed. Reading, Mass.: Addison-Wesley, 1990.

AMES, PATRICK. *Beyond Paper: The Official Guide to Adobe Acrobat.* Mountain View, Calif.: Adobe Press, 1993.

BANN, DAVID, AND JOHN GARGAN. *How to Check and Correct Color Proofs.* Cincinnati, Ohio: North Light Books, 1990.

BAUDIN, FERNAND. *How Typography Works and Why It Is Important.* New York: Design Press, 1989.

BLATNER, DAVID, KEITH STIMELY, AND ERIC TAUB. *The Quark XPress Book.* 3d ed. Berkeley, Calif.: Peachpit Press, 1993.

BRINGHURST, ROBERT. *The Elements of Typographic Style.* Point Roberts, Wash.: Hartley & Marks, 1992.

COHEN, LUANNE SEYMOUR, RUSSELL BROWN, LISA JEANS, AND TANYA WENDLING. *Design Essentials.* Mountain View, Calif.: Adobe Press, 1992.

COHEN, LUANNE SEYMOUR, RUSSELL BROWN, AND TANYA WENDLING. *Imaging Essentials.* Mountain View, Calif.: Adobe Press, 1993.

DAY, ROB. *Designer Photoshop: From Monitor to Printed Page.* New York: Random House, 1993.

ELLIS, RON, AND CHRISTOPHER BOTELLO. *Color Across America Seminars Guide Book.* Cambridge, Mass.: Thomas Munroe, 1992.

FINK, PETER. *How to Make Sure What You See Is What You Get! Expert Tips for Success in PostScript Output.* n.p.: Peter Fink Communications, 1992.

MCCLELLAND, DEKE. *Macworld Photoshop 2.5 Bible.* San Mateo, Calif.: IDG Books Worldwide, 1993.

NYMAN, MATTIAS. *Four Colors/One Image: Getting Great Color Output with Photoshop, QuarkXPress, and Cachet.* Berkeley, Calif.: Peachpit Press, 1993.

RICH, JIM, AND SANDY BOZEK. *Photoshop in Black and White: An Illustrated Guide to Reproducing Black-and-White Images Using Adobe Photoshop.* Berkeley, Calif.: Peachpit Press, 1994.

SOUTHWORTH, MILES, AND DONNA SOUTHWORTH. *Color Separation on the Desktop: How to Get Good Color Reproductions.* Livona, N.Y.: Graphic Arts Publishing, 1993.

SPIEKERMANN, ERIK, AND E. M. GINGER. *Stop Stealing Sheep & Find Out How Type Works.* Mountain View, Calif.: Adobe Press, 1993.

WILLIAMS, ROBIN. *How to Boss Your Fonts Around: A Primer on Font Technology and Font Management on the Macintosh.* Berkeley, Calif.: Peachpit Press, 1994.

WILLIAMS, ROBIN. *The Mac Is Not a Typewriter: A Style Manual for Creating Professional-Level Type on Your Macintosh.* Berkeley, Calif.: Peachpit Press, 1990.

WILLIAMSON, HUGH. *Methods of Book Design: The Practice of an Industrial Craft.* New Haven: Yale University Press, 1985.

Index

transferring, 5, 70–71

filters, work efficiency and, 7

flatbed scanners, 14–17

flatness, 6, 85–86

fonts. *See also* type

    actual size vs. point size, 58

    archiving and, 72

    cache, 5

    components, 56

    custom. *See* multiple master
      typefaces

    font metrics files, 56

    hard disk space and, 64

    PDF files and, 67–68

    PostScript operator for, 102

    printer's search for, 55

    in system setup, 5

    typefaces vs., 54–55

    working with a print vendor
      re:, 94

G

GATF Star Target, 96–97

Gaussian blur, 43, 48

GCR (gray component replacement) ink generation, 82

gradients

    CMYK mode and, 29

    trapping, 89, 91

graininess, 18, 48

graphics. *See* images

grayscale

    converting color images to, 48

    color correction and, 29–30

    color proofing and, 96

    dot gain and, 79

    making selections in, 7

    RGB scan of, 15

    trapping gradients on, 89

H

halftone screens

    editing PostScript code for, 109

    in printing process, 76

    resolution, 12, 19

    settings, separations and, 78, 84

    working with a print vendor
      re:, 94

hard disks. *See also* compact discs

    capacity vs. speed, 5

    optimizing, 5

    space, fonts and, 64

hardware recommendations, 5

high-end drum scanners, 14–17

highlights, 32–33, 35

histograms, 24, 31

HSB values, matching color via, 47

hues, 29, 47

hyphenation, 59

I

Illustrator. *See* Adobe Illustrator

images. *See also* photographs

    acquiring, means of, 10–11

    combining via layers, 44–46

    converting, 11

    drag-and-drop tips, 47

    extracting from PDF files, 68–69

    interpolation of, 23

    key type and, 30–31

    Kodak Photo CD, 11, 15–17, 24

    pixels and bits, 10

    resampling, 7, 22, 23

    resizing, 19, 22

    resolution. *See* resolution

    scanning. *See* scanners

    trapping. *See* trapping

Info palette, 24

interpolation, 23

J

justification, 58

K

kerning, 57

keyboard shortcuts, 7. *See also*
    specific function

key type, 30–31

Kodak Photo CD images, 11, 15–17,
    24

L

layers

    combining images via, 44–46

    dodging and burning with, 51

    trapping and, 90

    work efficiency and, 6, 7

leading, 58

letterspacing, 56–57, 59, 62

Levels command, 33–34

ligatures, 59

lighting, proofing and, 96

linear gradients, 91

line length and spacing, 58

M

memory

    system setup and, 4–5

    virtual. *See* virtual memory

    work efficiency and, 7

menu items, changing names,
    109–110

microline resolution targets, 97

monitors

    calibrating, 7, 8

    resolution. *See* resolution

    setup for printing, 8, 77

    work efficiency and, 7

multiple master typefaces. *See also*
    type

    described, 54, 61

    design axes, 61–63

    font names, 63–64

    managing, 64

    memory usage, 55

    primary fonts, 61

    printer compatibility, 61

N

native scan rate, 18

Nearest Neighbor interpolation,
    23

networks, using Acrobat on,
    70–71

neutrality, importance in color,
    29–30

O

object-oriented images, 10. *See
    also* images

old-style figures, 60–61

Open Prepress Interface, 106

operators, PostScript, 101, 102,
    104

optimizing disks, 5

outline fonts, 54. *See also* fonts

overprinting, 86, 87, 96

P

painting tools, paths and, 42

paper type

    dot gain and, 80

    tone reproduction and, 33

Pathfinder Trap filter, 87, 92

paths

    clipping paths, 86

    making selections with, 42

Colophon

Production Essentials was designed and produced using Adobe Photoshop, Adobe Illustrator, Adobe Streamline, Adobe Type Manager, and QuarkXPress on Macintosh Quadra 950 and Power Macintosh 8100/80 computers.

Typefaces from the Adobe Type Library were used throughout, with Minion, Minion Expert, and Myriad multiple master the primary fonts for text.

Laser proofs were printed on a Varityper® VT 600, an Apple LaserWriter Pro, an Apple LaserWriter II, a Canon® CLC 500, and a Kodak ColorEase™ PS Printer, all with Adobe PostScript RIPs.

Metagraphics, Palo Alto, California, produced scans, film, and proofs. Images were scanned on a Crosfield® MagnaScan and a Scitex® Smart 340 scanner (some scans on pages 15–17 were done on a low-end desktop scanner). Film was printed at 150 lpi on an Adobe/Scitex RIP with a PixelBurst™ coprocessor using Adobe Accurate Screens™ and a Scitex Dolev™ imagesetter. Color proofs were made using the Fuji Color Art proofing system.

Kodak Photo CD images were scanned using Kodak Photo CD technology. Color separations for these and other digital images were produced using the following Photoshop Preferences settings. Ink Colors: SWOP (Coated); Dot Gain: 22%; Separation Type: GCR; Black Generation: Light; Black Ink Limit: 100%; and Total Ink Limit: 310%.

The book was printed by Shepard Poorman, Indianapolis, Indiana, using the following equipment and materials: Fuji FND plates, Heidleberg six-color CD presses, and Kohl & Madden inks. Text pages were printed on 100-lb Corniche Velvet Book. The ink rotation was KCMY and the ink densities were set at K: 1.60; C: 1.25; M: 1.28; and Y: 0.90. Expected dot gain was 22–25% in the midtones.